All the Fullness of God

All the Fullness of
GOD

THE CHRIST OF COLOSSIANS

Bonnie Bowman Thurston

CASCADE *Books* · Eugene, Oregon

Cascade Books
An Imprint of Wipf and Stock Publishers
199 W. 8th Ave., Suite 3
Eugene, OR 97401

www.wipfandstock.com

PAPERBACK ISBN: 978-1-5326-1539-9
HARDCOVER ISBN: 978-1-5326-1541-2
EBOOK ISBN: 978-1-5326-1540-5

Cataloging-in-Publication data:

Names: Thurston, Bonnie Bowman, author.

Title: All the fullness of God : the Christ of Colossians / Bonnie Thurston.

Description: Eugene, OR: Cascade Books, 2017 | Includes bibliographical references.

Identifiers: ISBN: 978-1-5326-1539-9 (paperback) | ISBN: 978-1-5326-1541-2 (hardcover) | ISBN: 978-1-5326-1540-5 (ebook)

Subjects: LCSH: Bible. Colossians—Criticism, interpretation, etc.

Classification: BS2715.2 T48 2017 (print) | BS2715.2 (ebook).

Manufactured in the U.S.A.

An earlier version of chapter 4 appeared in *Restoration Quarterly* 41 (1999) 45–53. Used by permission.

Contents

Contents

Preface and Acknowledgments

There are many reasons for writing about a book of Scripture. One might, for example, be honored to be asked to contribute to a commentary series. One might need to write a book in order to be tenured at an institution. This is, perhaps a slightly venal reason, but a realistic one nonetheless. Or, one might write on a book of Scripture for the sheer joy of it, because she loves a particular book and what and whom it reveals. The volume in your hands is in the last category.

I have been intrigued by the book of Colossians for a long time, even before I wrote on it in connection with Ephesians and 2 Thessalonians.[1] I've wanted to devote a full-length study to Colossians, although, as a matter of discipline, I didn't go back and consult that earlier work in writing this one. So if you read it and find different opinions here, please conclude that I've changed my mind. A couple of years ago after a "zero birthday," I realized with a shock I'd better get this book written. I do so in the shadow of several excellent commentaries, which have influenced my thinking, in particular those by James D. G. Dunn, Eduard Lohse (in translation), Margaret MacDonald, Petr Pokorny, Christopher Seitz, and Jerry Sumney. Although this is not a verse-by-verse commentary, I am profoundly grateful for and have learned a great deal from these works which are.

The scholarly questions surrounding Colossians are extraordinarily interesting. Is this the last letter written by Paul or the first of the deutero-Pauline canon? In either case it is a "hinge" book in the Pauline corpus and reflects the application of Paul's think-ing to new situations. Who was behind the contrarian teaching, the teaching opposed to the church's founder, Epaphras, of whom the author approved, as he did of the Colossian church? What are the formal characteristics and theological and philosophical precedents of the famous "Christ hymn" in 1:15–20? Did the let-ter originate in baptismal catechesis? And what about the use of Greco-Roman literary forms in the second parenetic (practical teaching) section of the letter (3:1—4:6) or of Colossians apparent literary relationship to Ephesians?

This book doesn't officially weigh in on all of those questions. While it alludes to many of them, it focuses instead on the ca-nonical text as we have it (as does Seitz's commentary), concen-trating on what we do and can know, and not speculating over much about what is hidden in the mists of history. In part, this is because I think Colossians is a text for our times as well as for first-century Asia Minor. It approaches the person of Jesus Christ, and christological thinking generally, from a cosmological and cosmic perspective. It addresses questions of the Christian's behavior in a morally and ethically pluralistic environment as well as the matter of prayer practices and piety. How much that is of non-Christian origin should be imported into a Christian's spiritual life? This is a question for Christians in any age, but is clearly in focus in Colossians.

Most importantly, Colossians addresses the perennial cen-trality of Jesus Christ, who in the letter is the standard against which all else is measured. This Christocentricity was asserted in a world of cultural, philosophic, and religious pluralism not unlike our own. The letter focuses on the effect of baptism not only as "washing away" individual sin, but in a cosmic context, as allowing the "breaking in" of the "kingdom of the beloved Son" precisely through those he has "transferred from the dominion of darkness." (1:13–14) The Colossian writer envisions Christians as "little out-posts" of the Kingdom of God.

As noted, this work is not a verse-by-verse commentary. While I am indebted to the scholars who have written wonderfully helpful works in that form, I have decided to treat in essay form what I hope are logical units of Colossians in hopes that might give the reader a more synthetic understanding of the movement of the mind of Colossian's author. It was a most remarkable mind and produced a tightly reasoned and carefully organized letter. The first half of my book addresses in five chapters many (but not all) of the major scholarly matters in the letter. In that way it introduces the author's intentions with regard to the church in Colossae. Part II of the work consists of nine reflections on the text by way of demonstrating how the historical, linguistic, and technical issues have spiritually practical relevance for contemporary readers. Throughout I have attempted to minimize technical jargon and to make the author's very dense and rich text comprehensible to the general reader. The tone of my book is, therefore, consciously conversational.

For more than twenty years I have been intrigued by this letter that describes so clearly not just the importance of the resurrection of Jesus Christ for an individual, but its cosmic implications for the whole of creation. What we see alluded to in earlier of Paul's letters is worked out in more detail here (especially in the two theological centers of the work which I take to be 1:13–20 and 2:6–15). I am struck by the number of ideas from the Roman letter (which was not a surprise) and from Galatians (which was) that reappear in Colossians.

Over the past twenty or so years I have learned a great deal from students in my courses on Paul, and particularly on his Prison Epistles (at Lexington Theological Seminary and Pittsburgh Theological Seminary) and an exegetical course on Colossians at Emmanuel Christian Seminary. At Pittsburgh Seminary, the advanced Greek students and I spent nearly a year translating the text. In the summer of 2008, the congregants at Chapel Hill Christian Church in Brooke County, West Virginia, endured my preaching through the whole letter. It was a joy to give a series of lectures on Colossians at the 2016 Scripture Institute at Misericordia University (one of the hidden gems of biblical learning in the United States). In the autumn of 2016, a sizeable group of adults at St. Matthew's

Episcopal Church in Wheeling, West Virginia, gave their Wednesday evenings to serious study of Colossians. Perhaps the most personally powerful and affecting work I did on Colossians was early morning (as in about 4 a.m.) *lectio divina* on the letter at an extended residence at Our Lady of the Angels Monastery, a community of Cistercian nuns in Virginia. I have learned a great deal from all these saints (and from those who have written seriously on Colossians over the years), and grown enough as a Christian to admit that any errors of interpretation or theology contained herein are my own. I have tried to be scrupulous in citing ideas not my own, but having worked with the material for so long, it is possible that I have inadvertently overlooked a reference. I should be glad to be made aware of this in order to correct my error.

Finally, I offer most sincere thanks to the staff at Cascade Books of Wipf and Stock and especially K. C. Hanson for accepting this work for publication and for their great patience in helping a not adept computer user prepare her manuscript and for their editorial wisdom and expertise.

Bonnie Thurston
Wheeling, West Virginia

NOTES

1. Thurston, *Reading Colossians, Ephesians and 2 Thessalonians.*

PART ONE

1

"The Word of Truth, the Gospel"

Paul and the Church at Colossae

(1:1–12; 1:24—2:5; 2:8, 16, 18; 4:3)

INTRODUCTION

Unless you are a nerdy New Testament scholar, the letter to the Colossians is not highly likely to be in the center of your spiritual consciousness. And that's too bad because the letter focuses on issues that are of perennial importance to Christians. All the central ideas in Colossians revolve around Jesus Christ: the meaning of Christ in an individual believer's life, in the whole creation or the cosmos itself, and on the relationship of Christian believers to other religious practices, to what in theological circles is called "dual belonging," what is disparagingly described as syncretism.

In the interest of full disclosure, and as a nerdy New Testament scholar, I have to confess I love the Colossian letter and, happily, have had the opportunity to spend a good deal of time with it over the last twelve years or so, including doing a full translation of the epistle. Here's why I like it so much: without ever denigrating a personal relationship with Jesus, the Colossian letter throws open the doors and windows to show us just how far reaching are the implications of the incarnation, life, death, and resurrection of Jesus. The passion and resurrection of Jesus include, but mean so much more than, "personal salvation." Colossians shows us the cosmic Christ, the Christ who is too big to be contained by human documents and dogmas, the Christ who indwells everything, who made it all and keeps it all in being. That's the Jesus Christ I hope you glimpse in these essays on Colossians and experience in your daily life.

The whole theological shooting match (which, unfortunately it often is) aside, in the context of Pauline studies Colossians is a fascinating letter in its own right. Here is how James Dunn opens his 1996 commentary on Colossians: "Colossians could fairly be described as the most intriguing of the Pauline letters. This is primarily because it serves as a bridge between the undisputed Paulines and those members of the Pauline corpus generally considered post-Pauline." He continues, "Colossians shows us how Pauline thought developed, whether in the late phase of his own career or . . . among his close disciples after his death."[1]

Dunn reminds us that Colossians is a bridge, or I would say a "hinge" in Pauline studies; it holds together the seven letters that are generally assumed to be written by Paul (Romans, 1 and 2 Corinthians, Galatians, Philippians, 1 Thessalonians, Philemon) and those whose authorship scholars debate (Ephesians, 2 Thessalonians, 1 and 2 Timothy, Titus). Colossians "bridges" them in that, along with Ephesians (which seems literarily to depend upon it; Eduard Lohse wrote that "Ephesians reads like the first commentary on Colossians"),[2] reputable scholars are almost equally divided about whether Colossians was written by Paul near the end of his life or by a close associate or associates very soon after his death. For example, Mary Rose D'Angelo argues that it was the first step in the creation of a Pauline "school" and provided the format for the various warnings in 1 Timothy.[3]

The question of Colossians' authorship introduces the major scholarly centers of attention in the letter. The interrelated matters of authorship, the literary relationship between Colossians and Ephesians, the introduction of new literary forms, the identity of the so-called "opponents," and the presence in the letter of new theological trajectories have been of particular interest to scholars. Work on several of these subjects has involved historical speculation and the introduction of ideas *not explicitly evident in the text of the letter itself.* Those of us who have worked seriously on the letter have, of necessity, spent a lot of time with extra-textual matters.

Bear with me for just a minute. During my work on Colossians I was asked to review Christopher Seitz's commentary on Colossians in the Brazos Theological Commentary series for *The Catholic Biblical Quarterly.* It's a series that focuses on the theological relevance of biblical books and believes that Christian doctrine does not distort but clarify their interpretation. The series' general editor notes: "The central premise in this commentary series is that doctrine provides structure and cogency to scriptural interpretation."[4] In his introduction to Colossians, Seitz (who, interestingly, is an Old Testament/Hebrew Bible scholar) presents his general operating presuppositions. Two are relevant to this book. First, "the Bible exists in relationship to a community" and that community in history determines the questions that might appear a book.[5] Second, "the canonical presentation has its own kind of significance."[6] That is, the canonical text as we have it significantly affects what we can know of the author's intended meaning and places limits on our interpretation. These two ideas have affected how I'll present Colossians.

In thinking about how to acquaint you with the wonderful, but complex and much argued over book of Colossians, I wondered what would happen if I ignored, or at least downplayed the traditional questions of authorship and the identity of opponents and so forth. What if we ignored the speculative questions and dealt instead primarily with the canonical text as we have it? What would the text itself reveal about those first-century Christians? And how would that inform our own understanding of what it means to be a Christian? What I'm proposing to do in this study of Colossians is to deal with the text as text, to unpack some (but not nearly all!) of what it tells us. To do that responsibly it seems to me we need to know about the setting of the letter (about the town of

Colossae, and here, of course, we have to use sources outside the text), the reason why the letter was written (which is explicit in the text), and something of its structure, which we can discern by examining it carefully. That comprises chapter one. Then we will look at other features in the letter: its christology or focus on Jesus (chapter two) and its parenesis or practical advice (chapter three). Then using a *People* magazine or *National Inquirer* "inquiring minds want to know" approach, we'll see what we can learn about associates of the writer mentioned in the letter (chapter four), and, finally, we'll be in a position to consider the spiritual meaning of Colossians for today.

THE SETTING OF COLOSSIANS

The Ancient City: Geography

As I was thinking about Colossae at the time of the writing of the letter it struck me that it is rather like Wheeling, West Virginia, near where I live, or any other of a number of small cities in the American "rust belt." Colossae had been a more bustling and thriving place *before* than it was when the letter was composed, sometime in the late second half of the first century (if one holds Pauline authorship) or perhaps even very early in the second century (if one thinks Colossians is pseudonymous).

Colossae was in the southern part of ancient Phrygia in Asia Minor (modern Turkey) on the south bank of the Lycus River. It was ca. 110 miles east of Ephesus and 10 miles east of Laodicea on the main trade route from Ephesus to the Euphrates river. It is mentioned by ancient historians (Herodotus, Xenophon, Pliny, Strabo, Cicero) in connection with its location and trade, and in connection with the armies of Xerxes and Cyrus of Persia. Herodotus tells how Xerxes' army was stopped in its march on Greece (fifth century BC) and calls Colossae a "great city." A century later Xenophon described it as "a populous city, both wealthy and large." Figs and olives were grown in the fertile valley that supported sheep whose wool was woven and dyed to a red wool known as "colossinum." Strabo groups it with Aphrodisias as a major city.

The Ancient City: Demographics and Religions

It is significant that the cities of the Lycus valley had substantial Jewish minorities. Philo says Jews were very numerous in every city in Asia Minor."[7] Cicero notes there were 11,000 Jewish males there.[8] Josephus'[9] records that Antiochus III brought in several thousand Jews from Mesopotamia and Babylon in the second century BC.[10] Luke records that residents of Asia and Phrygia were in the crowd in Jerusalem on Pentecost (Acts. 2:9–10), and Laodicea is one of the cities mentioned in the Revelation to John. (Rev 3:14–22).

Colossians was nothing if not cosmopolitan. Evidence suggests that in Colossae the cult of Cybele, worship of Isis, and Mithraism (which appears wherever there is a Roman army presence) were practiced. Numismatic evidence points to worship of Ephesian Artemis (whose great temple was in nearby Ephesus), Laodicean Zeus, and other Greek deities as well as Egyptian Isis and Serapis.[11] And there were certainly Jews there who, like Paul, had become followers of Jesus. All of this led to a general atmosphere of syncretism, the blending of religious traditions, that the central part of the letter addresses.

By Roman times, however, Colossae was much diminished in size and importance. This was in part due to the fact that nearby Laodicea became the seat of Roman administration, and Hieropolis became known for its healing waters. There was a devastating earthquake in the Lycus Valley in AD 60 or 61 (near the time of Paul's death), which probably further led to the decline of Colossae. Oddly to my mind, the site has never been excavated by archaeologists, so it is hard to guess what the exact population was or what buildings of the city might have been like except from careful examination of written sources several of which, of course, occur in our New Testament.

THE FOUNDING OF THE CHURCH

The background of the Christian community in Colossae is found in Acts 19 and records of communities that Paul founded in Asia Minor during the time of his Ephesian ministry (about AD 52 to 55). Though we have no direct witness to this effect, Christians who belonged to those communities probably brought the Good News to Colossae, Laodicea, and Hierapolis (Col 2:1; 4:13, 15). Paul was not personally involved in missionary work in the area. The British New Testament scholar, Lightfoot, suggested that Colossae was the least important church to which an epistle of Paul was addressed.[12]

It is clear from the text of the letter that Epaphras brought the Gospel to Colossae (1:7–8; 4:12–13). Both Col 4:12 and Phlm 23 ("Epaphras, my fellow prisoner in Christ Jesus . . .") seem to suggest that he was with the writer of the letter. The text of the letter indicates that the early Christian community in Colossae was very diverse. There are frequent allusions to the "formerly estranged" (1:21), which I take to be a reference to the estrangement between Jews and Gentiles. Some Colossian Christians were "dead in trespasses and the uncircumcision of your flesh" (2:13), a clear reference to Gentiles who, we will see, had a fair number of things to learn to "put away" or avoid (3:5, 8). So the churches there included former Gentiles (probably of a variety of religious affiliations, what we now call "multiple belonging"), Jews, and perhaps syncretistic Jews. The Colossian letter challenges all these groups with regard to understanding the full implications of their (relatively new) faith in Jesus the Christ.

THE OCCASION OF THE LETTER

This brings us to the matter of the occasion of the letter. Why was it written? James Dunn provides an exact summary: "to counteract teaching that might become or already was either attractive or threatening to the baptized in Colossae, particularly with regard to their appreciation of the full significance of Christ."[13] I remind you that the presence of inaccurate or incomplete teaching does not necessarily mean the presence of an organized opposition to Epaphras and the Pauline gospel.

Let me point out at the outset that the general attitude of the author toward the Colossian church is positive. They are "saints and faithful" (1:2), known "for their faith and love" (1:4). They have "heard the word of truth" which is bearing fruit among them (1:6). They are "rooted and built up" in Christ and "established in the faith" (2:7). The writer of this letter admires the Colossian church (2:7). Colossians is not primarily about a confrontation over false teaching like that we find in Paul's letter to the Galatians in which the apostle is over-the-top upset with that church, or even like the polemical section of 2 Corinthians (which I take to be chapters 10–13 of that letter). I think many scholars have tended to read Colossians in the light of Galatians to the detriment of the former. As Victor Paul Furnish notes, however, this letter is "more admonitory than argumentative"; this is a "letter of exhortation and encouragement."[14]

The writer of the letter refers to the church's founder, Epaphras, as "our beloved fellow servant," "a faithful minister of Christ" who has "made known to us your love in the Spirit" (1:7–8). Although if the writer is Paul he hardly needs to be reminded, Epaphras has probably (note I am speculating here) made known to him the dangers inherent in the pluralistic environment in which the church exists. I am uneasy about cavalier references to "the Colossian heresy" because at the time the letter was written there *was* no "orthodoxy" in the sense of an adjudicatory body that determined belief and practice for the whole church. Indeed, Dunn points out "that the term 'Christianity' itself had not been coined . . .[15] This new movement was still in the process of defining itself. The "identity markers" for its adherents were baptism in the name of Jesus and confession of his Lordship. A lot of other stuff was up for grabs!

Scholars who think the author is confronting a pre-Gnostic "philosophy" have to work very hard to find in Colossians the systematic philosophical dualism that is necessary to posit a Gnostic outlook. The text itself does suggest that some of what worries the letter writer in the Colossian church has Jewish features: circumcision (2:11–13; 3:11), Sabbath (2:16), diet and purity rules (2:16, 21). But, one could hardly call this "heretical" since the church was "made up initially of Jews and God-fearing Gentiles or proselytes, some of whom would have been drawn from the synagogue."[16] I'm also uneasy with the idea of "Jewish syncretism" for the simple reasons that the Jewish community wanted and had the legal right to maintain its distinct religious identity and, in any event, had long since been influenced by Hellenism as the outstanding two-volume work on the New Testament by Helmut Koester (with whom I had the privilege of studying at Harvard Divinity School in the 1980s) so elegantly demonstrates.[17]

While I used to think it was *necessary* to the interpretation of Colossians to isolate a single, organized opposition to Christianity in Colossae, Gnostic, philosophic, or Jewish, I have changed my mind.[18] (I exemplify Maggie Smith's immortal line in an early episode of the television series *Downtown Abbey*, "I am a woman; I can change my mind as often as I choose.") Oceans of ink have been used in arguments for one or the other or some hybrid of these three groups as being the "false teachers."[19] Such theories draw their evidence primarily from 2:6–23, in which it is well nigh impossible to reconcile all the various data into a single so-called opponents' position. Maybe that's because there *wasn't* a single, unified, opponent. I'm not the first, or the smartest, person to propose this.

Some years ago, Morna D. Hooker (a scholar whose work I greatly admire) wrote an article titled "Were There False Teachers in Colossae?" in which she points out that most commentators assume an attack on false teachers. Then she raises what I think is the key question. *If* there is false teaching in Colossae why doesn't Paul (or the author) attack it with the vigor he uses in Galatians? She points out that the young Colossian Christians were surrounded by moral laxity to which the regulations of Judaism must have provided an alternative. Similarly, the Colossian environment assumed the existence of supernatural powers from which one needed to be protected. No false teachers were required to prove their existence. Hooker believes Paul's primary concern is the young Christians' relationship to Christ, not to false teachers. The Colossian Christians were under pressure to appropriate practices of their pagan and Jewish neighbors. But such practices were unnecessary because both creation and redemption are completed in Christ.[20]

More recently, in a chapter titled "The So-Called Conflict at Colossae (2:8–23)," Christopher Seitz has also, on the basis of text of the letter, argued against a single opponent of Pauline teaching in Colossae. He writes "The alternatives in my view do not belong to a single religious system . . ." And later, "Less obvious is whether they [the various terms used to describe the alternative view in Colossae] all refer to a single system threatening the Colossian Church."[21] He believes that the "point of the strong commendation in 2:5–7 . . . is to establish what is true . . ."[22] Seitz helpfully and creatively sets up his commentary on 2:8–23 in terms of "factual" and "counterfactuals," not in terms of Pauline Christianity and "opponents" of various stripes.

Personally, I think (at least for today) the Colossian letter was occasioned by the writer's need to remind the Colossian church that the Christ into whom they were baptized and whose Lordship they claimed is the all-sufficient answer to their spiritual searching and needs. The letter reminds them of what they learned from Epaphras (1:7): that Jesus Christ is all-powerful in the universe whose agent of creation he was and also provider of answers to all human quests and questions. The letter was written for a christological purpose that we shall explore in greater detail in the next chapter.

THE STRUCTURE OF THE LETTER

Colossians follows the general pattern of a first-century letter and the one that is customary in Paul's uncontested writings. Dunn calls it "characteristically Pauline in its structure," with "the features that cause most surprise" being the "substantial development of the thanksgiving" and "the incorporation of household rules into the parenesis."[23] That pattern is as follows:

1:12	Opening formula (sender, addressees, greeting)
1:3–12	Thanksgiving (3–8) and prayer (9–12)
1:9—4:6	Body: doctrine/theology (1:13—2:23) then parenesis/practical teaching (3:1—4:6)
4:7-17	Greetings to friends and associates (unusually extensive)
4:18	Closing formula

I think a bit more precision in examining the body of the letter (1:9—4:6) will be clarifying, so I suggest the following divisions and include Lohse's explanations. He describes 1:12–23 as the first "instructional portion" and 3:1—4:6 as the second "hortatory portion . . . equally determined by the theme of the universal dominion of Christ."[24]

1:15-23	Addresses the Sufficiency of Christ. 1:15–20 is a Christ hymn, which in 1:21–23 is applied to the community.
1:24—2:5	Describes the author's or Paul's ministry. (In Philippians, the discussion of Paul's ministry also precedes a Christ hymn.)
2:6-23	Addresses the author's concerns about the Colossian Christians.
3:1—4:6	In light of Christ, this section describes what is to be "put off" and "put on," and "demonstrates how in reality obedience to the Kyrios ought to be carried out."[25] The famous (or infamous!) "Household Code" in 3:18—4:1 is to be understood as part of that teaching.

Lohse concludes his presentation of the letter's structure: "Just as there is the unfolding of the universal scope of the dominion of

Christ in the first two chapters of the letter, the third and fourth chapters give an exposition of the ways in which the lordship of Christ includes all areas of our life. Teaching and exhortation are thus closely bound to one another."[26]

Another way to think about the structure of Colossians is suggested by the divisions in Jerry Sumney's excellent commentary. He suggests that after the epistolary greeting (1:1–2) and introductory thanksgiving and prayer (1:2–23), the letter has three arguments:

> Argument 1: Accept This Letter's Teaching and Instruction because Paul Is the Trustworthy Bearer of the True Gospel 1:24—2:5.
>
> Argument 2: Accept This Letter's Teaching and Instruction because Only This Message Is Consistent with the Faith You Have Already Received 2:6–23.
>
> Argument 3: Accept This Letter's Teaching and Instruction because You Have Been Granted Holiness in Baptism 3:1—4:6.[27]

In order to fill out our knowledge of the backgrounds of Colossians so that we can read the text more accurately and clearly, two brief excurses are in order.

EXCURSUS 1

The Literary Relationship between Colossians and Ephesians

Just as there is apparently an historical relationship between Colossians and Philemon by virtue of shared *dramatis personae*,[28] there is an apparent literary relationship between Colossians and Ephesians. Some 25 percent of Ephesians has direct parallels in

Colossians. Of 155 verses in Ephesians, 73 have parallels in Colossians. Structurally the two epistles are closely related in that one follows the other in order of presentation of material. Additionally, there are stylistic and lexical (vocabulary) similarities, similar themes and theological points of view, and perhaps a common fund of early Christian hymnody.

Not surprisingly there are different theories to explain the relationship between the two letters. Two basic scholarly positions are that Colossians functioned as a sort of draft for the writer of Ephesians or that Ephesians was written first and Colossians is an abridgement of it (the *Reader's Digest* condensed version?!?). The question of authorship enters into the debate. Some argue Colossians was one of the last letters Paul wrote, and Ephesians was written by one of Paul's disciples to address his church's contemporary situation. Some argue that neither epistle was written by Paul but both contain Pauline ideas. Fewer argue that both mutually depend upon a third document that we don't have (perhaps a sort of Pauline "Q" like the posited shared sayings source in Matthew and Luke's gospels).

Although the matter won't greatly affect our interpretation of Colossians, my own view is that Colossians was probably written first, and Ephesians follows it in chronology, literary style, and, for the most part, theology.

EXCURSUS 2

Deutero-Pauline Christianity and Pseudonymity

It is generally understood that associates of the disciples of Jesus recorded those disciples' memories of the action and teaching of the Lord. St. Luke, for example, tells us at the outset of his gospel that he wasn't an eyewitness, but recorded what was delivered to him from them (Luke 1:14). Something similar seems to have occurred in the community around the Apostle Paul. After his martyrdom, Paul's disciples applied his teachings to the communities he left behind and to those that they, themselves, founded. Those letters (and there is huge debate about exactly which they are) reflect the church's changing self-understanding in a changed socio-political environment. Evolutionary theory suggests that what doesn't change or adapt doesn't survive. I suggest this might be as true of institutions as it is of individual species (and individuals, as well).

By ca. AD 70 the original twelve apostles called by Jesus were probably dead. Paul had been martyred. The *parousia*, the return of Jesus, which the first generation of Christians had thought was imminent was obviously delayed. As a result, the work of the nacient Church became that of how to live in the Roman Empire and adapt to a longer "stay." Part of that work, as we've noted, certainly included the development of its required beliefs and practices, though it would be some time before that work was concluded (and some would say it is still in process). For our purposes it's enough to know that the disciples and followers of Paul took up this task and that of preserving Paul's teaching with modifications for their own time period and circumstances.

This leads us to the matter of pseudonymity, of writing in another person's name. The practice was not uncommon in the biblical world or in Greco-Roman literature. Somebody long after Daniel wrote a now biblical book in his name. Plato wrote as if he were Socrates. This would not have been considered either dishonest or plagiarism. It was considered a tribute to a master when a disciple tried to write as he had or reproduced his ideas. For example, letters circulated under the name of a teacher were believed to carry his authority. The issue then was not "making things up" or "deceiving," but preserving teachings, in the case of Paul, while modifying them for current situations, making Paul's teaching "relevant" by applying them to the church's new position. In the Greco-Roman world, pseudonymous writing honored the supposed author, applied his teaching to new situations, and gave his authority to a work written by someone else.

Some scholars have made the case that the following New Testament letters are pseudonymous: possibly Colossians, 2 Thessalonians, Ephesians, and the Pastoral Epistles (or at least 1 Timothy and Titus). These works have several themes in common. First, they are concerned with church unity and the marks of unity in belief and practice. Second, they deal with holiness of life; in them we see the beginnings of ethical codes, rules for Christian behavior and mention of how to restore to community the erring brother or sister. The third concern is apostolicity, which is really about the matter of authority. What happens when the original apostles die? Then who has authority, and how is it determined, and who can wield it?

Deutero-Pauline works, for example, were written to preserve that apostle's teaching and traditions. They have some noticeably different literary features from the works we think Paul probably wrote. The sentences are much longer. Meditations on one subject are interrupted by other things. We find in them fragments of early Christian hymns and liturgical material (indicating that the church was developing her worship traditions). The vocabulary can be quite different from Paul's, or Pauline terms can be used with meanings different from his own. And there are theological differences. These letters speak in terms of the "mystery of Christ," the reconciliation, not only of the whole cosmos through Christ's death and resurrection, but of Jew and Gentile as an accomplished fact. Christ has broken the divisions in the cosmos and those between people (see, for example, Eph 2:11–14). The image of the Church as the Body of Christ is extended to include His "headship." [29]

Historically, the early church had to come to terms with the destruction of the Temple in Jerusalem, the delay of the *parousia*, the increasing possibility of persecution, and the perceived threat of "pagan" (i.e. Gentile) ideas and practices creeping into Christian teaching and practice. Paradoxically, during this time we see in Christian literature increasing use of the ideas and vocabulary of Hellenistic religious traditions, philosophical literature, and its forms. And, because Christianity's roots are Jewish and many early Christians were Jews or God-fearers, Jewish Scripture and theology continued to be appropriated in various ways by the early Church. We see the reality of this in the Acts of the Apostles and in Paul's letters, particularly in Galatians and Colossians, in Paul's moral teaching in the Corinthian letters, and his theological teaching in Romans. Things were in flux. There didn't seem to be a normative early Christianity, so it was hard to say until many years later what was "heretical," a term I prefer not to use in relationship to New Testament works.

And right in the middle of all this is the book of Colossians, either one of the last books Paul wrote or one of the first ones his disciples wrote, and, in either case, a bridge between the two and between Paul's ideas and the changed circumstances of the early church. Many of its details link it with Philemon whose authenticity has never been questioned. And yet many scholars think its christology, ecclesiology, and *parenesis* are a stage beyond that of Paul. So I close this chapter, as I began, with James Dunn's assessment that "either way Colossians shows us how Pauline thought developed . . ."[30] In Colossians we are dealing with an extraordinary mind, one willing to expand the implications of what it knew and profoundly believed about Jesus Christ not only in the realm of personal religiosity, but into the far reaches of creation and the cosmos itself. Finally, I think that if we are to grasp something of the author's intentions, we must open our own minds to mystery of God's fullness revealed in Jesus the Christ.

2

"Your Faith in Christ"

The Theological Center of the Letter

(1:13—3:4)

INTRODUCTION

Colossians 1:13—3:4 comprises the transition from the thanksgiving of the letter (1:13-14) and the first and more theological teaching section in 1:15—2:23. There follows the second, more practically oriented teaching section of 3:1—4:6. Four units are discernible in 1:13—3:4. First, 1:13-14 describes what "the Father" who is the object of thanksgiving (1:12) has done for the Colossians: effected a cosmic transference into "the kingdom of his beloved Son." This leads to 1:15-20, the Christ hymn (with which we'll be primarily concerned in this chapter) which describes the extent of the son's authority and power. Third, 1:21—2:5 is the author's personal response to what he has been told about the Colossian Christians, and, fourth, 2:6-23 describes the relation of the Christic material to the recipients of the letter.

Colossians 1:13—3:4 has been the focus of a great deal of scholarly attention both because of the hymn and because this is the section which contains the material that has been used to try to define and characterize the "false teachers" in Colossae.[31] The oft quoted false teaching references include

2:4	"that no one may deceive you with plausible arguments"
2:8	"philosophy and empty deceit" and "elemental spirits of the universe" (which also appears in 2:20)
2:16	"matters of food and drink or of observing festivals, new moons, or Sabbaths"
2:18	"self-abasement and worship of angels, dwelling on visions"
2:20–21	"regulations. Do not handle, Do not taste, Do not touch"

It isn't to my mind necessary to pinpoint the origin of these teachings which the Colossian author finds misguided to understand that what is at issue is the Colossian Christians' understanding of Christ and what it means to belong to Christ, to be taken into Christ by baptism. In my view, what the author is doing in this section of the letter is more presenting the Colossian church with a fuller understanding of Christ, of the extent of his authority and power, than attacking their tendency to be purloined by alternative teaching which they are hearing. Note the tone of the writer's address to the fellow Christians he has not met ("have not seen me face to face" 2:1), but who "share in the inheritance of the saints in light" (1:12). The author has heard of their faith, its growth and fruitfulness (1:6) and is praying constantly for them (1:9). The author is "now rejoicing in my sufferings for your sake" (1:24). God's commission to him "was given to me for you" (1:25), and he wants them to know "how much I am struggling for you, and for those in Laodicea, and for all who have not seen me face to face" (2:1–2). He wants their hearts to be encouraged, their love united and their knowledge assured (2:2). The writer is apparently not particularly angered by an attack on his authority or teaching.

The Colossian church was founded on Epaphras' teaching of which he approves (see 1:1—3:14). He is sending Tychicus and Onesimus to "encourage your hearts" (4:8). Apparently the writer and the Colossians have many acquaintances in common (see 4:7–17; more on that in chapter four.) The writer of Colossians wants to deepen and nurture the understanding of the Gospel and of Christ which that church already has. The letter to the Colossians wasn't written so much to attack false teaching (as was, say, Galatians) as to expand the understanding of Christ. Unless I badly misread it, this is exactly what the writer told us in the opening thanksgiving prayer in 1:9–14.

I think the letter to the Colossians is about the beauty, majesty, and power of Jesus Christ and the relationship of that to how Christians live their lives. In what is neither a scientific or even computer generated study, I counted the references to Jesus Christ in Colossians, looking for references to "Jesus," "Christ," "Jesus Christ," "the Lord," "the head," or pronouns (he or him) whose antecedent is one of those proper nouns or titles. Here's what I came up with: Chapter 1 has 29 verses and 30 references to Jesus. Chapter 2 has 23 verses and 24 references to Jesus. Chapter 3 has 25 verses and 16 references to Jesus. Chapter 4 has 18 verses and 4 references to Jesus. That's 71 references to Jesus in Colossians, with the majority of them (about 51) in the theological teaching section. Even if my count is off, I think the lexical evidence clearly suggests what's on the author's mind, and it isn't in six isolated verses in the first two chapters of the letter. The Christ hymn with which the letter opens is the key to the whole epistle because it demonstrates that Jesus Christ is the ultimate authority and power in the universe.

THE CHRIST HYMN—
THE HEART OF COLOSSIANS

After the traditional opening formula (1:1–2), in the letter's thanksgiving (1:3–8) the writer seeks to establish friendly relations with people he hasn't met but of whom he has heard a positive report. The prayer for the Colossians in 1:9–12 asks that, on the basis of what God has already done for them, further benefits be added. The teaching in 1:13–23 can be subdivided into three units: vv. 13–14 outline what God has accomplished through Jesus Christ and speak in terms of God and "us," what God has done for "us;" vv. 15–20 are the Christ hymn and speak only of the Christ, and describe the agent of God's action; vv. 21–23 explain how the Colossians are affected by the facts presented in the hymn and how *they* should act in response. The author speaks to "you" (plural) and describes the hoped for effect of the action and its agent.

The fact that the writer and recipients of the letter figure in the "soteriological brackets" (vv. 13–14 and vv. 21–23), but not in vv. 15–20 are one of the things that suggest that those verses are an insertion. For scholars who hold Pauline authorship of the letter, so does an absence of articles, the piling up of participial phrases (relative clauses in English), and the non-Pauline vocabulary (10 non-Pauline expressions and 5 hapax legomena).[32] The critical literature on the hymn is voluminous and often technical.[33] I read that it has occasioned the most commentary of any passage in the New Testament, and I believe it.

Instead of burdening you with summaries of all that, let me tell you my conclusions. I think that the author of Colossians chose an existing hymn which is deeply rooted in the soil of the Wisdom tradition (especially the Wisdom of Solomon).[34] The following parallels provide evidence for that claim:

"He is the image of the invisible God . . ." (Col 1:15a)

"For she is a reflection of eternal light,
a spotless mirror of the working of God,
an image of his goodness." (Wis 7:16)

[He is] "the firstborn of all creation" (Col 1:15b)

"I will tell you . . . how she came to be . . .
I will trace her course from the beginning of creation" (Wis 6:22; see Prov 8:22 and Sir 24:9)

"... all things have been created through him and for him." (Col 1:16d)

"For he created all things so that they might exist." (Wis 1:14; see Prov 3:19–20)

"He himself is before all things, and in him all things hold together . . . For in him all the fullness of God was pleased to dwell." (Col 1:17, 19)

"Because the spirit of the Lord has filled the world, and that which holds all things together knows what is said . . ." (Wis 1:7)

These are but a few of the many parallels and verbal echoes of the Wisdom of Solomon in the Colossians hymn. Whoever wrote the epistle apparently knew Wisdom and Israel's wisdom tradition well.

Perhaps, as Käsemann has suggested, the hymn was from a baptismal liturgy. Baptism does figure highly in the letter. In any case the hymn was known to the writer and to the Colossians, and, with some of the author's emendations, makes the exact points he wishes to stress to improve their understanding of Jesus Christ. This is really very clever. The writer is not introducing new information into a situation that seems troubled by just that, but using something they *already* know to deepen their understanding, something they know from their own worship, something that is "in their bodies" so to speak, because they have sung or chanted it. Modern preachers quote hymns known to their congregations to illustrate their sermons for just these reasons. In pastoral work, I have encountered many examples of people who have forgotten what day it is, but who can sing from their damaged memories the hymns of their youth because they have "taken them in" so to speak.

The Structure of the Hymn

In vv. 15–20 there are several nominal sentences beginning with "he" (vv. 15, 17, 18). In two of these "he" is "firstborn" (vv. 15a, 18b) followed by the phrase "for in him" (the *hoti* clauses in vv. 16 and 19). The formula "from-through-to" also appears in Rom 11:33–35. These repetitions have led to two basic understandings of the structure of the hymn.[35] First, it has been understood to have two stanzas. Verses 15–18a deal with Christ and creation, and vv. 18b–20 deal with Christ and reconciliation. Or, second, it has been understood to have three stanzas: vv. 15–16 are about creation; vv. 17–18a are about its preservation, and vv. 18b–20 are about its redemption. Probably the more commonly accepted division is the two-part one, which seems more natural and exhibits a closer parallelism between the stanzas.

The Hymn's Assertions about Christ

However one understands the stanza structure of the hymn, it makes at least eight assertions about Jesus Christ which are critical to the Colossians' understanding of him. Verses 15 to 17 address Christ and creation and assert the following: 1) he is the image of the invisible God; 2) he is the firstborn of creation; 3) in him all things were created; and 4) in him all things hold together. Verses 18–20 make at least four assertions about the relationship of Christ to the church and the world: 5) he is head of the body, the church; 6) he is firstborn from the dead; 7) in him God's fullness resides; 8) he is the cosmic reconciler. The following material, in which I follow the two stanza form, examines in more detail at these eight assertions.

Christ and Creation (1:15–17)

1. Jesus Christ is "the image of the invisible God" (1:15a).
In Greek the word " image" is *eikon*, ikon. An "image" was understood to share the reality of what it represented (which is the basic

23

idea in the Orthodox Church's theology of icons). Jesus Christ is not a copy of God, but *is* God, participates in God's *morphe*, God's essence (as per the Philippian hymn, 2:6 of that letter). The frequent appearance of *ikon* in the New Testament suggests this concept must have been a fairly widely know and understood idea in the early Church. Hebrews 1:3 records that Christ bears "the exact imprint of God's very being." In 2 Cor 4:4 Paul writes of Christ "who is the image of God." This means that Christ not only makes God "visible," that is palpable or knowable to humans, but participates in the nature of God, stands with the Creator apart from the creation. (And see the quotation from Wis 7:16 above.) The next three assertions about Jesus clarify his relationship to the Creator and the creation.

2. Jesus Christ is "the firstborn of all creation" (1:15b).

This phrase contains the first of eight uses of forms of the word "all" (*pas*) in the hymn. The repetition indicates its all-embracing implications, its universal applicability. In a culture deeply steeped in the advantages of primogeniture, to be "firstborn" (*prototokos*) was of great importance (and, for example, accounts for a good deal of the anger of the disgruntled older son in Luke's "Prodigal Son" parable). Primogeniture conveyed a sort of sovereignty over other family members. Since in Hellenistic Judaism the *logos* is also called the first born, the phrase serves to introduce the whole Wisdom tradition into the hymn and bears out our earlier contention that there was a lively Jewish-Christian community in Asia Minor. Wisdom was personified as feminine (Proverbs 8; Ecclesiastes 24; Wisdom 7), "created before all things" (Prov 8:22; Sir 1:4), and present with God from the beginning (Wis 9:9). Wisdom shares the divine throne (Wis 9:4), and, in a complication of genders, Philo calls "her" the "firstborn son."

Prototokos speaks of primacy of function as well as priority in time. Christ holds primacy in and over the order of creation. This primacy is so important that it is mentioned at three other points in the hymn: v. 17 "before all things"; v. 18 "he is the beginning;" (in a rabbinic explanation of Genesis, *archai* is also a designation of the *logos*, a term of special relevance in early Christianity in

Asia Minor, as John's gospel also attests); v. 18 he has "first place in everything."[36]

3. In Jesus Christ "all things in heaven and on earth were created, things visible and invisible," "all things have been created through him and for him" (v. 16).

The dependent clause at the end of v. 16 modifies the last phrase of v. 15. In v. 16 the work of Christ in creation is described in the passive voice, suggesting that God was the *prima mobile*, the initiator, and Jesus Christ was the agent. The creation is "through Christ" (*di'autou*); the genitive makes Christ the means or instrument of creation. The repetition of "all things" in the verse indicates the extent of Christ's influence on creation. Everything, including all power and authority, whether temporal or eternal, visible or invisible, natural or supernatural find their origin in Christ. Jesus Christ (perhaps understood as the perfection of Lady Wisdom?) is the creative power of God by means of which God created everything that is.

4. In Jesus Christ "all things hold together" (v. 17).

In the Hebrew tradition, the whole creation, which originates in God and occurs by the agency of Jesus Christ, coheres or is held together by Christ. Think of Jesus Christ as the "Super Glue" of creation! This is not an entirely new idea. Around the second century BC, Ben Sira declared "by his [God's] word all things hold together" (43:26). The term "hold together" (*synestēken*) is used in Platonic and Stoic philosophy to describe the wonderful unity of the whole world. The point is that Christ sustains what he has created. This is not the universe of the Deists. God didn't create the universe and abandon it to its own devices, nor does God require of believers the sort of special practices which apparently tempt the Colossians.

To summarize, the thought in Col 1:15–17 sounds remarkably like that of Paul in 1 Cor 8:6: "For us there is one God, the Father, from whom are all things and for whom we exist, and one Lord, Jesus Christ, through whom are all things and through whom we exist." That verse strikes me as Paul's "Christianization" of the Shema (Deut 6:4). The language in these three verses echoes that of Greco-Roman philosophy. The hymn uses the language of philosophy to show how Christ triumphs over it (a Pauline technique we find in many other letters, and especially in Ephesians). It also seems to be filling in for Gentile believers in Asia Minor some of the Jewish theological tradition (in this case Wisdom) that was in the process of being used by early Christianity to understand and explain Jesus Christ. This same two pronged approach is used in the second half of the hymn.

Christ and the Church (1:18–20)

Having established the pre-eminence and supremacy of Christ in creation, the hymn turns to the relation of Christ to the church and the world, and asserts that he is head of his body, the church and firstborn from the dead. In him God's fullness dwells. He is the cosmic reconciler.

5. Jesus Christ is "head of the body, the church" (v. 18).

In a variety of Greek sources including Plato, the Stoics, and Philo, the universe is imagined as a body ruled by a head because, like a body, the universe needs a governing principle. It's important to note that "head" (*kephale* in Greek, *rosh* in Hebrew) does not necessarily connote "authority" as we now understand it so much as "source," or "point of origin," or "leader."[37] Unlike Paul's use of the "church as body" metaphor in 1 Corinthians 12 or Romans 12, here Christ is "head of the church." Several scholars think "the church" is the author's addition to the hymn and that this use was echoed by the writer of Ephesians. In any case, it underlines again Christ's Lordship over everything, and stresses two facts about him. First, it echoes earlier assertions that everything is from him; Christ is the ultimate "source," the point of origin of his body the church. (Thus the perennial questions "was Jesus married?" might be answered, "Yes. From the beginning to his bride the church.") Second, he therefore "rules" or leads (by primogeniture) everything in creation.

6. Jesus Christ is "the beginning, the firstborn from the dead" (v. 18).

This is the second use of "firstborn" (*prototokos*) in the hymn and reintroduces the complex of ideas around primogeniture. In a family the term "firstborn" is not normally used unless there is more than one child. Jesus is the first of those who will follow and signals a new creation since is he the first step in a more general resurrection which includes not only human beings, but all creation. This same idea appears in Paul in 1 Thess 4:13–18 and Rom 8:19–23. Christ is firstborn among many brethren and, if we are to believe Rom 8:19–23, the first in a making new of, a re-creation of the creation itself. Occurring together "beginning" and "firstborn" suggest the founding of a new people, a revitalization of the creation, and the promise that *others will follow*. The implications of Jesus Christ extend far beyond that of personal salvation alone.

7. In Jesus Christ "all the fullness of God was pleased to dwell" (v. 19).

In 15a Christ is described as the "image of God." Verse 19 asserts that God's fullness is pleased to dwell in him. The totality of divine power and grace, love and justice and mercy, all that we assert of God, resides, literally "settled down permanently" (*katoikesas*) in Jesus. "Fullness" (*pleroma*) is a particularly potent word. It means "completely full" and "mature."[38] John's prologue uses the term: "From his [the Word's, Christ's] *fullness* we have all received grace upon grace" (1:16, italics mine). In the language of religious syncretism of the time *pleroma* designated the uppermost spiritual world, the one closest to the deity, a sort of "buffer zone" between gods and humans, and as such was an intermediary to god.[39] It is an interesting *double entendre* as it is used here.

The writer of Colossian's point in beginning the letter with this hymn is precisely that such an intermediary is unnecessary since, in having Christ, the Colossian Christians *already* have God. They don't need to worry about "principalities and powers" (2:15) or "worship of angels" (2:18) or "elemental spirits of the universe" (2:20). The writer uses the language of the troublers against them. He takes their cosmology and turns it to Christian soteriology.

Chapter 2 vv. 9 and 10 provide the writer's gloss: ". . . in him the whole fullness of the deity dwells bodily, and you have come to fullness of life in him, who is the head of all rule and authority." What an extraordinary mind composed this letter!

8. Jesus Christ is the cosmic reconciler (v. 20).

Ruler of the universe and the church, Jesus Christ is the beginning of a new phase of creation. God's enormity resides in him, and so he is able to reconcile to himself everything, "making peace by the blood of his cross." Nothing in the universe stands outside the scope of Christ's reconciling work accomplished in his death on the cross and his resurrection by God. No alien powers, certainly none of those mentioned in Colossians chapter 2, can stand against Christ, his Church, and his people. Verse 20 moves the cosmological truths of vv. 15–17 into the realm of personal relationship; it speaks of "reconciling" and "making peace," but not just between people, but in every aspect of creation.

In Greek the word "reconcile" (*apokatallazai*) means to exchange hostility for friendship. The compound preposition at the outset (*apo-* "from" and *kata-* "down") indicates return to a condition or previous state that was lost. Jesus Christ, who was in essence God, restores the creation and its inhabitants to their original relationship with their Creator (whose agent he also was). And, ironically perhaps, he does this by "coming down" (Phil. 2:7–8). Likewise "making peace" (*eirenopoiesas*), the same root word in Matt 5:9 which blesses peacemakers as children of God, describes the means of this reconciliation. By his suffering and death on the cross, Jesus Christ has returned all things to proper relationship with God. Heaven and earth are brought back into the divinely created original order. And this reconciliation and peace *have already begun* in Christ Jesus.[40] And they have begun, as well, in those baptized into him.

To summarize, the Christ hymn in Colossians makes a series of assertions about Jesus Christ, most of which we find elsewhere in the New Testament. Because of the lexical field chosen,these assertions about Christ might also have been understood by students of Greco-Roman philosophy. I have indicated the philosophical principles at issue in brackets before giving another New Testament reference with the same or a closely related idea. Attentive readers will note how many of these ideas also occur in Johannine writings which share the cosmological assumptions of Colossians.

1. He is the image of the invisible God and perfectly reveals God. (2 Cor 4:4)

2. He is the firstborn of creation [Christ's primacy]. (John 1:1)

3. All things are created in and through him [Christ's agency]. (John 1:3, 10a)

4. He is before all things [Christ's temporal priority]. (John 1:1–2; Rev 3:14)

5. In him all holds together [Christ's principle of coherence]. (Heb 1:3a)

6. He is the head of his body, the church [Christ's origin and authority]. (Eph 1:22–23)

7. He is the first born from the dead, thereby cosmic reconciler [Christ's agency]. (Rev 1:5)

CONCLUSION

James Dunn's commentary on Colossians notes that Paul often puts christological formulas at the outset of his letters. The hymn and its framework at the outset of Colossians isn't polemical. Dunn notes "We may fairly deduce that Paul and Timothy thought the preeminence of Christ, in terms both of creation and redemption, needed to be emphasized. But the absence of polemic suggests that Christ's status and significance were being devalued rather than attacked, that an alternative religious system was being exalted . . ."[41]

The letter to the Colossians opens with this hymn because the writer, who had not met them, but had heard good things about them, also thought their understanding of Christ was not sufficient for the challenges they faced, challenges we can infer from 2:6–23.[42] In the Christ hymn in 1:15–20 the writer of Colossians provides the Colossian Christians with a conceptual framework with which to think about the "add ons" to their faith that are being suggested to them, in fact that seem to be being required of them by teaching other than that of Epaphras. These matters are alluded to primarily in 2:8–23. If you read 2:8–19 carefully, you will hear echoes of 1:15–20 which can only be intentional. The repetition in the hymn of forms of "all" eight times in five verses underlines that, whatever the issue is, Christ has it covered![43]

Immediately after the hymn, in 1:21–23 the writer (or Paul) begins to apply it to the letter's recipients with the emphatic "And you" at the outset of v. 21. "You" who were estranged, hostile and evil are now holy, blameless, and irreproachable because of the reconciliation Christ effected, so continue in, without shifting from the gospel you heard (v. 23). (This same idea is repeated in 2:6–7.) Presumably the Colossians heard the gospel from Epaphras, and this seems to remind the writer/Paul of his own work for the gospel, its sufferings and struggles and the fact that it is for others, matters to be taken up in 1:24 to 2:5.

I don't think we can know with any certainty the source or sources of the inadequate understandings of the Christian spiritual life that are alluded to in 2:8–23. Certainly they reflect an awareness that in the cosmos the visible and invisible worlds exist simultaneously. We, in fact, say this in the Creed: we believe in "all things visible and invisible." But, I'm not sure that most modern people have, in reality, this sense of "dual dwelling," that we live in both material and immaterial worlds simultaneously. In fact the writer presents the Colossians' choices in terms of dualisms, "either–ors." For example, 1:21–22 describes what they were before Christ and what they are after. Especially in 2:20–23 we see the choice set forth as alternatives: what is human vs. what is of God; the perishing vs. the eternal; the impotent vs. the powerful; the shadow vs. the substance; what is below vs. what is above. As William Hendricks notes, Colossians affirms that the only really clear communiqué from the invisible world to the visible is Christ.[44]

Similarly, I don't think the writer is opposed to individually chosen spiritual practices per se. What he opposes is human imposition of them on others as requirements (2:16, 18, 22). He knows that they are impermanent, temporal, perishing (2:17, 20, 22), that they don't empower human self-control (2:23), and, most importantly, in the light of Jesus Christ's sufficiency, they are not necessary for those "in Christ" (2:17, 19, 20). The writer is warning the Colossians about optional additions to the essential gospel of Christ they have received. The basic thing that I think the writer wishes to stress in this first block of teaching material is the freedom the Christian has "in Christ" because of Who Christ is and what Christ has done. Although without the polemic of that letter, I think he would agree with Gal 5:1: "For freedom Christ has set us free; stand fast therefore, and do not submit again to a yoke of slavery." Both Paul and the writer of Colossians know that the most terrible slavery is spiritual or religious in nature.

The sad fact is that people like to be told what to do. It saves us from having to think for ourselves. In the gospels, Jesus faces this matter. For example, on "the other side of the Sea of Galilee" (John 6:1) when commanded "Do not work for the food that perishes . . ." (John 6:27) the crowds whom he had fed immediately ask Jesus "What must we *do* to perform the works of God?" (John 6:28, italics mine). And after the first Christian sermon ever, which was about the nature of what God had done through Jesus, not what *people* must do, the hearers "said to Peter and the rest of the apostles, 'Brethren, what shall we do?" (Acts 2:37). This section of Colossians reminds us that ultimately Christianity is not about what we do, but about what has been done for us and whether we have the strength of character to set aside the falsity of human self-sufficiency for a heavenly humility that accepts what has been given. We are "in Christ" not by good deeds, acts of will, moral courage, intellectual acuity, or physical asceticism but by submissive acceptance of what has been done for us. This is "the mystery that has been hidden throughout the ages and generations, but has now been revealed . . ." (Col 1:26).

There is much of scholarly interest in this section of Colossians. The following excurses treat only two matters, one (apparently shocking) theological statement by the author and one lexical matter with theological consequences for the recipients of the letter.

EXCURSUS 3

Completing What Is Lacking in Christ's Suffering? (1:24)

Careful readers of Colossians will find 1:24 startling on at least two counts. First, the author (if not Paul, the thought here appears frequently in his uncontested letters), rejoices in suffering, an unusual response to that experience. Second, the verse apparently suggests something is lacking in Christ's afflictions or suffering. To add to the confusion, the verse contains many lexical anomalies.[45] We might dismiss the problems by suggesting that perhaps the writer/Paul *did* think there was something less than perfect that he was bringing to completion. The problem might be ours, who labor with 2,000 years of theological work in christology that the early church and the Colossian writer didn't have. The church fathers did not seem as troubled by the verse as have modern commentators who have devoted sustained attention to it.

The first apparent difficulty is the more easily resolved, although it is intrinsically related to, the second. "I am now rejoicing in my suffering for your sake" is a succinct statement of a theme found in Paul's undisputed letters, that of rejoicing in suffering which characterizes the apostle's ministry (see, for example, Rom 5:3; 12:12; 1 Cor 4:9–13; 2 Cor 2:1:5–7; 7:4; 11:23–27; Gal 6:17). And, for example in 2 Tim 2:3, the author suggests Timothy "share in suffering like a good soldier of Christ Jesus."[46] As a nonconforming minority group in the Empire, now exempt from the protection of the *religio licita* of Judaism, suffering was the lot of the early Christians.

But that is not the issue here in Col 1:24 where several matters of translation are of importance. First, the pronoun "my" does not occur in the Greek text, so one might conclude that what is in view are Christ's sufferings except that they are "for you," so they must refer to the author's suffering.[47] Second, the preposition "in" (*en*) could mean both "in the midst of" or "because of." Third, the word "suffering" (*thliphis*) here could be translated "pressure," "suffering," or "tribulation." Commentators point out that it is never used in the New Testament of the sufferings of Christ. And that alone may speak to the apparently christological problem.

Sumney (whose readings of this verse I have found most persuasive and helpful) notes that in Colossians "Paul's sufferings play a more central role than in most other Pauline letters."[48] They "help establish his authority" in a church he has never visited.[49] The author's sufferings are "for you," i.e. "for your sake." The author has accepted suffering for the sake of the Colossians whom he has not met. Dunn points out that for Paul "suffering meant suffering with Christ, sharing Christ's sufferings (Rom. 8:17; 2 Cor. 1:4, 4:10–11; Phil. 3:10–11)."[50] The writer's suffering is "for the sake of [Christ's] body, that is, the church;" it both cements his authority and makes him an example to be emulated. MacDonald elegantly suggests "Colossians 1:24 offers a window into the intense religious experiences of an early church community: one detects a profound sense of interconnectedness among believers, community, cosmos, and Christ."[51]

So far, so good. But what of the phrase "completing what is lacking in Christ's afflictions"? The word translated "completing" comes from a rare verb *antanapleroō* (two prepositions, *anti* and *ana,* affixed to the verb *pleroō,* which shares the root with *pleroma,* "fullness," earlier discussed in the Christ hymn) which means "to fill up." Commentators point out that to take the phrase literally contradicts what was said in 1:13–14, 22 and what will be said in chapter 2. And to constrict the implications of Christ set forth in 1:15–20 destroys the argument being subtly made against those who suggest something more *is* required. Bruce is correct: "The present context rules out any suggestion that the reconciliation effected by the death of Christ needs to be supplemented."[52]

Then what might it mean? Interpretations of the phrase include that Paul's suffering is edifying, but does not supplement Christ's expiatory death; that Paul's sufferings *are* the sufferings of Christ because of Christ's mystical union with believers (we will revisit this idea in chapter 5); and that what must be in the author's mind are Jewish apocalyptic literary traditions suggesting the righteous must suffer before the end. (See, for example, Jesus' own "apocalyptic discourses" in Mark 13:9–37 or Matt 24:1—25:46.) The more a single righteous person suffers, the less suffering will be required of others.[53]

I, personally, find Sumney's solution to the theological problem the most persuasive and satisfactory. While not ignoring the apocalyptic tradition, he reads the verse in light of Greco-Roman understanding of the suffering and death of noble persons. My own sense is that Colossian Christians might have been more aware of Greco-Roman thought (like that of Seneca) than of Jewish apocalyptic. Seneca, for example, teaches that good people suffer in order to teach others to endure and to serve as a pattern to be imitated. Martyrs, in particular, are to be imitated (as 4 Maccabees 79 vividly illustrates from the Jewish tradition). Vicarious suffering, suffering for others, can have an expiatory function (as did Christ's) or a mimetic function (as did the author's/Paul's). "Paul's sufferings are indeed vicarious, but not expiatory. The death of Jesus alone remains expiatory, but Paul's sufferings can truly benefit others."[54] In the context of Colossians, Paul suffers for the Colossians' benefit to provide a model for imitation. "The Colossians' mimesis is to take the form of obedience to Paul's gospel and the commands he gives in the letter."[55]

One final note might be worth pondering. The day after the Feast of the Exaltation of the Holy Cross (September 14), the church invites us to keep the memorial of Our Lady of Sorrows. As we do on Good Friday, we see our Lady at the foot of the Christ's cross. One of the daily office prayers records "his mother Mary stood by him, sharing his sufferings." If anyone "filled up" or "completed" Christ's sufferings, surely it was his mother, Mary, who did not turn aside from that suffering and demonstrated in an essential way how Christ's people might share it. The prayer continues, "May your church be united with Christ/in his suffering and death/and so come to share in his rising to new life."[56]

EXCURSUS 4

"The Record That Stood against Us" (2:14)

Jerry Sumney's commentary on Colossians points out that in 2:14–15 there are three words that appear only here in the New Testament, three that appear nowhere else in the Pauline letters, and one that appears only once elsewhere.[57] The untypical vocabulary is for some scholars part of the evidence for non-Pauline authorship. I would suggest that whomever the author, the task at hand requires a specialized and unique vocabulary. The material in 2:8–15 first reiterates ideas from the Christ hymn (vv. 9–12) and then illustrates by means of a series of striking metaphors the power of God manifest in the forgiveness of sins by means of Christ's death on the cross (vv. 13–16). One of these images is found in the *hapax legomenon* "*cheirographon*" which the NRSV translates "the record."

Literally a *cheirographon* was "a document written by the person responsible, a holograph."[58] One might translate it "handwriting," and Sumney explains that its nonreligious uses "often designated a record of a debt."[59] It is modified by the dative *dogmasin* which carries the idea of a formal decree (from the Greek *dogma*, "decree"), some official announcement or proclamation. The image may be that of the cancellation of a debt or bond, "the certificate of indebtedness issued by the debtor in his or her own hand as an acknowledgment of debt."[60] Although at least one scholar has wondered whether the *cheirographon* represents Christ,[61] I think the idea carried by the metaphor is that the cross cancels a record of debt. The *cheirographon* is a metaphorical way to speak about forgiveness.

There exist in Jewish apocalyptic texts references to a book in which heavenly beings have recorded the deeds of human beings. For example in the *Apocalypse of Elijah* an accusing angel holds in his had a book in which sin is recorded; the book is a record of sin used in the condemnation of human being.[62] The *Apocalypse of Zephaniah* speaks of guilt and the wiping clean of this book. Revelation 20:12 alludes to heavenly lists of human deeds.[63] Margaret MacDonald convincingly suggests that in Paul's letter to Philemon Paul's promise, written in his own hand, to discharge any debts Onesimus has accrued (Phlm 18–19) also reflects a certificate of cancellation of a debt and that the language here in Colossians would have deeply affecting resonances for other slaves in the Christian community.[64]

Use of the term *cheirographon*, then, is an example of the way the writer of Colossians appeals both to those of Jewish heritage as well as of Gentile. Ralph Martin suggests it is a statement of obligation written by a debtor to pay what is due, here used as a personalized allusion to the charge list of guilt which Christ assumed in his body and over came by his cross.[65] This official, handwritten decree of sin and indebtedness, God has wiped out or erased (*exaleiphas*) by means of Christ's death on the cross.

In vv. 14 and 15 God is the primary actor who effects a literary and legal cancellation of debt by "nailing it to the cross." (Ralph Martin suggests these verses are a "picturesque and dramatic account of the events of Good Friday."[66]) Then the author then employs a series of military metaphors to describe how God disarms (or strips) the "rulers and authorities," and triumphs over them, an image of the Roman triumphal procession, the victory parade that displays the spoils of war and humiliates the defeated.[67] And the means of the debt cancellation and the triumphant victory is the cross of Christ. As Dunn points out, in v. 14 the cross is an image of destruction and in v. 15 an image of public triumph. "To treat the cross as a moment of triumph was about as huge a reversal of normal values as could be imagined, since crucifixion was itself regarded as the most shameful of deaths."[68]

The unique vocabulary in vv. 14 and 15, and in particular the word *cheirographon,* is chosen to mirror the unique power and authority of God over the "elemental spirits of the universe," (the *stoicheia tou kosmou,* a phrase used deprecatorily by Paul in Gal 4:3[69]) who have, themselves, already been "taken captive" (*sulagogon,* itself a rare word meaning, literally, "made captive" or "carried off as booty"). The writer frames 2:8–16 with images of the captivity of and triumph over any forces in the universe opposing God and Jesus Christ. Sumney says it best: "In vv. 6–15, Christ is the means by which God works; the one in whom the fullness of deity resides; the one in whom believers receive forgiveness of sins, new life, and fullness; and the one in whom the readers live and are rooted and founded."[70] This is why teaching opposed to that of Epaphras is "empty deceit" (2:8) and the practices to be described in the immediately following passage (2:16–23) are unnecessary for the Colossian Christians. The death of Christ, through which God has forgiven sin and blotted out its debt, also cancels the need for them.

3

"Raised with Christ"

Put to Death, Put Away, Put Off, Put Up

(3:1—4:6)

INTRODUCTION

I've suggested that the writer of Colossians wanted to warn that Church about un-necessary do's and don'ts. Don't be made a captive to philosophy and deceit (2:8). Don't be condemned in matters of food, drink, and festivals (2:16). Self-abasement (what we might term asceticism) or the worship of angels (2:18) are not required of Christians. Be wary of those who insist on ascetic practices and "regulations" (2:20–22). Now in this second block of teaching material (3:1—4:6) we apparently have rather a lot of just this sort of thing. The writer is apparently afraid the Colossian Christians will lapse back into the Power of Darkness from which Christ has delivered them (1:13). So this teaching section of Colossians is dominated by the implicit comparison between what they were then (estranged, hostile, and evil, 1:21) and what they are now (holy, blameless, and irreproachable, 1:22) and by the imperative mode. What's the difference between what was condemned in the previous material in 2:8–23 and what is discouraged or encouraged in this one?

First, on the historical level these detailed instructions may have to do with the demographics of the Colossian church and with the possible origin of the letter. In a comprehensive and helpful overview of 3:1—4:6, Roy Yates points out that similar parenetic (teaching) material was collected and used in the church before Paul.[71] In Christian communities made up of Jewish and Gentile believers, or in primarily Gentile communities, because they did not know Torah, the moral assumptions would have been very different from those of Jews. (As, for example, were their differing dietary practices as Acts 15 demonstrates.) The early church had numerous cultural differences to bridge and knew it, which is why its early spokesmen often focused on the reconciling work of Jesus (see, for example, 1:20, 22). Ethical instructions were necessary for Gentiles (and undoubtedly for some Jesus Jews as well), and we find them not only in Paul's letters, but in 1 Peter and James.[72]

Second, I mentioned in the discussion of the hymn in 1:15–20 that some commentators (notably Ernst Käsemann) have suggested that parts of Colossians originated as a baptismal liturgy or instruction. They note that 3:1–17 echoes some of the language that Paul uses about baptism in Romans 8. The phrase "being raised with Christ," for example, is probably not metaphorical, but a description of the newly baptized being raised from the waters of baptism which was in the early church by immersion as *baptizo*, "to dip" suggests. Those to be baptized literally "took off" their old clothes (and metaphorically their old natures), and "put on" new robes (and hopefully new natures) after their baptisms. Images of taking off, putting on, and "clothing" dominate 3:5–17 which is a teaching about the consequences of baptism, we might say of becoming Christian, for ordinary life and behavior.

I think both of those suggestions have merit, and that there are even deeper, more human and spiritual reasons why the warnings in 2:1–23 are different from those in 3:1—4:6. In an article on the latter in *Review and Expositor*, C. F. D. Moule begins by movingly pointing out that in Colossians the announcement of Good

News preceded the challenges of the Christian lifestyle. Before the demand is made, the gift is offered. Another way to say this is that Christian exhortation is sacramental before it is ethical. For Moule, it is the sharing in the death and life of Christ in baptism in 2:20 and 3:1 that forms the presuppositions of the ethical instruction in the letter. The "if" (*Ei*) at the beginning of 3:1 assumes that they *have* been raised with Christ. (The Greek construction presumes the affirmative response.) The exhortation addresses those *already* Christian.[73]

If 2:8–23 warns against what is temporal and unnecessary, 3:1–17 presents what is enduring and important for the Colossian Christians. Practically I think the difference is that of from outside in or from inside out, from what is imposed versus what is chosen and voluntary. What the writer of Colossians objected to in the first block of teaching was the notion that beliefs beyond that in Jesus Christ and practices or actions that Christ did not require were, in fact, being presented as *necessary*.[74] (A parallel situation is reflected in 1 Tim 4:1–5.) If you want to think in terms of false teachers, think that their teaching was that things were necessary and required other than confession of Jesus as Christ and baptism.

The second block of teaching material in Colossians assumes that the recipients are Christians and describes appropriate responses to the gift given and received in the life, death, and resurrection of Jesus. They are being exhorted to *choose* to behave in certain ways as a *response* to what has been done for them. Having been buried with Jesus Christ in baptism, they are asked to conform their way of life to his. Glen Hinson suggests that "Faith frees but love binds the Christian."[75] The Christian has great freedom, but is bound by love to certain courses of action. We'll have occasion to say more about this when we examine the household code later in this chapter.

Many Christian people have the experience of the joy of having chosen some difficult task because they love the one for whom it is being done. The things one does for a dying spouse or a religious community member might be wretchedly difficult and would be abuse if one were *forced* to do them, but when *chosen* for love's sake, they become a source of deep joy, even gratitude. Parenthetically, I think this is one of the things that Jesus means when he asks his disciples to take up their crosses. Taking up a cross is about conscious choice and chosen action, not passive acceptance of what comes ones way in life. And on that note, we turn to literary matters in 3:1—4:6.

STRUCTURAL AND LITERARY FORMS

Colossians 3:1—4:6 is a synthetic unit of didactic material or parenesis. It is difficult to divide it into sub-units because one teaching flows smoothly into the next in a logical order. However, one might use the literary forms as a way of demarcating units of teaching. The "traditional materials" in Colossians (which also appear in some of Paul's undisputed letters, certainly in Ephesians and the Pastoral Epistles, and in the books of Peter and James) are literary forms that were used in Greco-Roman moral and ethical teaching that some writers of the New Testament adapted for Christian use. The seminal work on traditional material in Colossians was done by George E. Cannon in his book *The Use of Traditional Materials in Colossians* (1983).[76] My thinking in what follows is indebted to his work and to that of Roy Yates, whom I've previously mentioned.

Cannon suggests that based on the United Bible Society's text of Colossians, of 114 lines in the first two chapters, thirty-four (30 percent) are drawn from traditional materials and twenty-five are careful application of them.[77] There are at least three types of traditional material in Col 3:1—4:6: vice and virtue lists, *topoi*, and a household code. Using these traditional materials as points of demarcation in 3:1—4:6 suggest the following units: 3:1-4 (which provides the theological rationale for what follows); 3:5–14 (primarily a collection of vice and virtue lists dominated by the metaphors of "putting to death" [3:5], "putting off" [3:9], and "putting on," clothing metaphors in 3:10, 12, 14); and 3:15-17, and 4:2-7 (collections of *topoi*, brief, pithy admonitions sometimes on unrelated topics) which frame what scholars have described as a "household code" in 3:18—4:1. What follows in this chapter explores these units.

Theological Rationale and Its Practical Consequences
(3:1-4)

Honestly, I'm not sure whether these verses were intended as the conclusion of 1:24—2:23 or the introduction to 3:1—4:6. They can certainly be understood as the hinge holding the two units together. The Colossian Christians have been warned off "life style" requirements, but are now being given teachings that stress comparison between the amoral, earthly life (3:5-9) and the virtuous, heavenly life (3:12-17). As previously noted, the comparison is between what they were before baptism and what they are becoming as a result of it. They are to "seek the things above" (3:1) because "above things" have permanence that the life style injunctions of which the Colossian Christians were warned don't. This principle of holding to what is enduring or permanent is profoundly Pauline. Although in Greco-Roman literary format, the following teachings originate with Christ who is "above," "seated at the right hand of God" (3:1), the place of authority. The permanence of "above things" (*ano*) echoes Platonic ideas as well as the Pauline notion that the earthly or fleshly is impermanent. *Sarx*, flesh, is not evil but ephemeral, impermanent. (This point has been widely and frequently misunderstood.) It may be that the opposites in 3:2 echo those suggested in 2:8-23.

Colossians 3:3 echoes 2:20 in its declarative rather than conditional mode and lifts up the great post-baptismal, mystical reality: the Christian's authentic life is a hidden one. (Our Lady is the perfect example of this, as are the lives of many quiet, little people, the *micron* in our parishes.) Just as the image of "Christ within" is used in the letter (1:27, for example), now the believer is "in Christ" (see also 2:6-11). Like God in Psalm 139, you can't get away from Jesus Christ (as Rom 8:35-39 also asserts). The word for "hid" or "hidden" (*kruptō*) means "concealed," "covered," "kept secret." It is in passive voice suggesting that this is a hiddenness that is gift, conferred, done to one. Verse four implies that Christ's hiddenness may be only for a season; then he will be revealed, with his followers, in glory (compare Luke 17:30; Rom 8:19; and 1 John 3:2). What follows is an elaboration of the moral and ethical "earthly realities," the practical consequences of baptism, of having died, been raised with, and hidden in Christ who, in a "geographical conundrum," is also within (more on that point in chapter 5).

The Clothing Metaphor, Vice/Virtue Lists, and Topoi (3:5–17)

The teaching in this section is dominated by the metaphors of "put to death" (3:5), "put away" (3:8), "put off" (3:9), and "put on" or "clothe" (3:10, 12, 14). This image was widely used in the ancient world, especially in the Mystery religions to describe initiations and spiritual change.[78] It is used by Paul in Rom 13:12 and 14. I suspect the Colossians use is a baptismal image that carries over from the first section of the letter (and compare Rom 6:1–14). I am quite sure it echoes a teaching method used both by Hellenistic Jews and the Stoics and thus is especially appropriate to Colossians' diverse Christian community. It's called the "Two Ways." Think of it as "on the one hand/on the other hand" teaching. (We in the West are familiar with it as it is used so frequently in advertising to sell us stuff. "This is your laundry before this detergent, and this is your laundry *after*.") Here it is suggested the Colossians can choose the path of holiness or that of perdition. They were not so lovely before baptism. Now they can choose something else. That the "Two Ways" was a popular early Christian teaching method is borne out not only by the New Testament, but by its appearance in *The Didache* 1–6 and *The Epistle to Barnabas* 18–20.

Vice and virtue lists are another literary device found in Greco-Roman ethical teaching, especially that of the Stoics, and are also widely used in the New Testament (see, for example, 1 Tim 6:11).[79] They are exactly what they sound like and are the vehicle the Colossian author uses to present his "Two Ways." Cannon points out that the vice/virtue lists in Col 3:5–12 are some of the most tightly structured in the New Testament.[80] Each of the three lists of five has a central focus. Verse 5 is a vice list with a central focus on sexual sins (with possible reference to the Holiness Code of Leviticus 18). "Walked" in v. 7 is a common Pauline metaphor for "lived." The Colossians used to live in ways which bring God's wrath (3:6–7 and compare Rom 1:18).

Verse 8 is a vice list with a central focus on detriments to personal relationship. The attitudes of anger, wrath, and malice lead to sinful forms of speech like slander and abusive (literally "filthy") language. Since one normally doesn't tell people not to do what they aren't doing (unless one wishes to put ideas in their heads), presumably the Colossians were doing these things, too. But they have "stripped them off" and "reclothed" themselves "according to the image [*ikon*] of [the] creator," that is, according to the image of Christ (3:9–10). The repetition of the word "image" from the Christ hymn suggests that the Colossian Christians, too, are "God carriers." The description of the remarkably diverse demographic of the Colossian church in verse eleven (an abbreviated version of Gal 3:28 which also occurs in the context of a vice/virtue list) belongs with vices that destroy community. Having an "us and them" attitude, privileging racial or ethnic divisions hinders Christian unity. There can be no social or cultural or racial divisions in Christ because Christ is in all Christians (1:15–20, 27; 2:13), and all Christians dwell in him (3:3). (Our contemporary social crises are indicative of the fact that we Christians have not begun to live out the practical implication of this mystical fact of baptism. For more on that idea, see the reflection on this text in Part Two of this book (pp. 83–130).

Verse 12 is a virtue list that echoes the qualities of Jesus, himself, and provides specific examples of how to build and to be in relationship to fellow believers, even those with cultural differences as great as those among Greeks, Jews, barbarians, Scythians (nomads and the ultimate barbarians[81]), slaves, and free persons. The essential quality of forgiveness highlighted in verse thirteen mirrors in human relationships the great reconciling work of Jesus in the cosmic realm which was depicted in the hymn in 1:15–20.[82]

(In the Colossian letter one is never very far from the Christ hymn.) Not surprisingly, the virtue lists move toward love (3:14) the cardinal Christian virtue, and peace (3:15), the theological virtue that is to "rule" the heart. The word for "rule" (*brabeuō*) is a verb that means to act as a judge (legal metaphor) or an umpire (sports metaphor). If peace "calls the shots" in the heart (for Greco-Romans the center of person and the origin of volition or will), the whole person will be properly ordered. Note that thankfulness and gratitude (two words from the same Greek root) are repeated in the successive three verses (vv. 15–17), thus emphasizing those attitudes.

Following from verse fifteen, the writer has begun a series of short admonitions that culminate in verse seventeen with a summary suggestion that everything, whether in word or deed should be done in Jesus' name (which stands for Jesus, himself).[83] Apparently in verse sixteen we get a little glimpse of early liturgical practice which included word, teaching, admonition of one another, singing (cf. 1 Cor 14:26). It's also possible that verse fifteen both summarizes the previous vice and virtue teaching and begins the *topoi* that are resumed in 4:2–6. *Topoi* are, as noted, brief admonitions on a single or a series of different topics often strung together by catch words.[84] Interestingly one can read 3:17 and skip to 4:2 without experiencing disjuncture. That and the high incidence of *hapax legomena* (words that occur nowhere else in the New Testament) in 3:18–4:1 has led some scholars to suggest it was a separate unit of material inserted at this point in the letter (rather like the Christ hymn in 1:15–20 seems to be an insertion of earlier material).

Household Relationships in Christ (3:18—4:1)

Extensive work has been done on the famous (perhaps to some modern ears infamous) "household code" forms, which also appear in Eph 5:21—6:9 and 1 Pet 2:18—3:17 and are reflected in 1 Timothy. The seminal work on this material is James E. Crouch's *The Origin and Intention of the Colossian Haustafel* (1972),[85] and interesting discussions of the "code" are found in *A Feminist Companion to the Deutero-Pauline Epistles.*[86] Excellent background material on the Greco-Roman family is found in *Families in the New Testament World*, a readable and accessible study by Carolyn Osiek and David L. Balch.[87] Here, we will only introduce the lively conversation on the household codes, and will confine our discussion to its purpose in this letter.

Although scholars disagree, many think that the form, itself, originates in popular Hellenistic ethical teaching.[88] For example, Aristotle taught that the domination of the male over the female led to a properly functioning household and, ultimately, to a properly functioning state.[89] Philo also linked household and state management. The concept of familial duty is clear in Stoic teaching, and the principle of relational reciprocity was known in Seneca. Keep in mind that the stability of the Greco-Roman household was intrinsically linked in the popular mind with the stability and proper functioning of the society. The domestic was political. A threat to the household was a threat to social order. (We still hear this in some contemporary ethical rhetoric and teaching.)

In the Colossians code (which is shorter than the one in Ephesians, and more developed than the one in 1 Peter) there are three sets of reciprocal exhortations arranged from closest relationship to least close: wives/husbands (vv. 18–19); children/fathers (vv. 20–21); slaves/masters (3:22—4:1). E. Glen Hinson (whose reading of this passage I greatly admire) suggests that the key theme throughout is "mutual submission and mutual love."[90] The first party addressed in each grouping is subservient to the second, and only the subordinate parties are given theological motivation for their actions ("as is fitting in the Lord," v. 18; or "this is your acceptable duty in the Lord," v. 20).[91]

It interests me that the code contains the highest concentration of references to Jesus in the second half of the letter: one in the teaching to wives (v. 18); one in the teaching to children (v. 20); four in the teaching to slaves (vv. 22, 23, twice in 24); and, interestingly, once in the closing reminder to the master that *he* has "a Master in heaven" (4:1). This is a subtle but startling reminder that the master's behavior should be like that of his heavenly master, Christ, who died for *both* human masters and slaves. In fact, it is noteworthy that the instructions in the code place limits on each of the more powerful figures, which in fact would generally have been the same person, the *pater familias*.

Clarice J. Martin points out that the essential concern of the code was for the relationship of the weaker to the dominant figure.[92] The longest exhortation here is to slaves (3:22–25) and in all the other New Testament codes to slaves and wives. This indicates a special interest in slaves within the Christian household. (And see instructions about slaves in 1 Tim 6:1–2 and Titus 2:9–10.) The interest in slaves is undoubtedly because early Christian communities included many slaves, and their relationships with their Christian masters would have been, to say the least, complex, especially in light of Jesus' teaching that "whoever would be first among you must be slave of all. For the Son of man also came not to be served but to serve . . ." (Mark 10:44–45). We can't be sure the Colossian Christians would have known sayings of Jesus (and, of course, Mark's gospel probably hadn't yet been written), but that both masters and slaves were by virtue of baptism "in Christ" would certainly have changed society's accepted power dynamic within the Christian community. And that would have been true as well of the marital relationship in a patriarchal culture. As the work of Scott Bartchy has demonstrated, slavery in the Greco-Roman world bears little relationship to slavery in the ante-bellum American South.[93] Nevertheless any reading of the code that supports human bondage is a grave misuse of the text.

Why, then, does it appear here? I think it has to do with the position of Colossian Christians in their social and cultural environment. As this second teaching section demonstrates, when people became Christians, their behavior was expected to be different from that of non-Christians. They are no longer what they were before baptism. The parenesis in the letter assures us of this. But some twenty-first-century Americans are not the first society to conclude "different" might mean "dangerous." The first-century Christian minority challenged several widely accepted

47

social paradigms. Ideally, in the church the disciples of Jesus didn't scrupulously follow society's patriarchal norms (perhaps because, as later gospel narratives indicate, Jesus didn't). More equitable relationships with women or wives or slaves (of either sex) would have been perceived in the wider society as a threat, a cause of disorder. If the household is the root of the social order, and Christian households were "unusual," then they were also threatening or at least potentially threatening to social order. Greater reciprocity in relationships might have been grand within the Christian household and community, but also put that household and community in a precarious position in the wider society.

James Crouch's study of the matter concluded that the original purpose of Christian household codes was to serve as a curb to threats the "freedom in Christ" represented to the safety and stability of the church in the social order. Similarly, Clarice Martin notes that disciples of Jesus didn't respect patriarchal bonds, and this threatened existing society and had to be limited.[94] I am glad I was not a leader of one of the Christian communities in a Greco-Roman environment (not Chloe in Corinth, Nympha in Laodicea, or any one of a number of women Paul greets in Romans 16) and had to sort out the tension between freedom "in Christ" and threat both to and from the social order. What do you do if "freedom in Christ" leads to behavior that draws unfavorable attention to the minority Christian community, attention that would threaten the very existence of that community? Those, I think, were the stakes.

Final Parenesis (4:2–4 and 5–6)

With 4:2 we pick up the *topoi* left off at 3:17. If the household code were an insertion, the author was clever to frame it with instructions on spiritual and liturgical practice (3:16–17) and prayer (4:2–6). Whether one sees the code with modern eyes as patriarchal and restrictive or with first-century eyes as wonderfully liberal (and perhaps dangerous), it is disturbing. And what disturbs should lead the Christian to prayer, as, indeed, the Colossian letter now does. Verses 2 to 4 are *topoi* on prayer, and verses 5–6 can be understood to summarize the whole parenetic section. It is characteristic of Paul to close a letter with a series of short commands that include instructions on prayer. (See Rom 15:30–33; 2 Cor 13:7–9; Eph 6:18–20; Phil 4:4–7; 1 Thess 5: 16–18, 23, 25.) Because we are going to look at Colossians' prayer texts in more detail in chapter 5, I will pass over 4:2–4 and focus on the *topoi* in 4:5–6 which summarize the parenetic section 3:1—4:1.

While 4:5–6 might seem to be random imperatives, their unifying focus is the behavior, and thus reputation, of the Colossian Christians in their social context (and so they are, in fact, closely related to the household code). They suggest that those relations may be less than completely irenic. There are three instructions. First, conduct yourselves wisely toward *outsiders*. Second, make the most of the time. And third, let your speech *always* be gracious (italics mine). Each has implications for how Christianity would appear to outsiders, a matter of great importance to Paul, and to those who applied his teachings in later letters written in his name and addressing different and perhaps more precarious times than did the Apostle.

To conduct oneself wisely toward outsiders might well mean to behave in ways that will not draw negative attention to the community. First-century communities were much more *communal* than ours in the contemporary West. What an individual did reflected on his or her family or community. "Conduct yourselves wisely" in the Greek is *hen sophia peripateite*, literally translated, "walk in wisdom," a lovely admonition. As noted, "walk" was a favorite Pauline metaphor for how one lives, one's "lifestyle." (See, for example, 2 Cor 5:7 or Gal 5:2.) One wonders if this is an oblique reference to the Wisdom traditions in which the letter's christology is grounded. Certainly Christ is a wisdom figure in this letter, so we may have here another "in Christ" reference.

If the imperative is to "live in Christ like Christ" toward non-Christians, it's a big order, and one that underscores the difference between Christian communities and their context, serves to protect it in its minority status, and functions as an evangelistic or missionary tool. Who would not be attracted by one who behaves as Christ toward him or her? If this reading of verse 5a has any legitimacy, then 5b, "make the most of the time," would mean something like "seize the opportunity" by witnessing with your lives. In their *Linguistic Key to the New Testament*, Rienecker and Rodgers point out that "time" (*kairos*) "does not emphasize a point of time but rather a time space filled [with] all kinds of possibilities."[95] "Make the most of the time" may also be an oblique reference to belief in the nearness of the Parousia (the return of Christ). Certainly Paul expected Christ's return (see, for example, 1 Thess 4:13–18 and 1 Cor 10:11), so it is not unreasonable to suggest that teachings on the Parousia would have been part of the Pauline gospel Epaphras brought to Colossae. Perhaps the idea is "make the most of the time, saints; there may be less of it than you think."

Remember the command to gracious speech in verse six is given to a community with internecine "mouth troubles" as 3:8–9 attest. Once they "clean up their language" and learn to speak with grace to one another, they must turn that skill toward outsiders. The parenthetical phrase "seasoned with salt" modifies "gracious," and suggests their speech is not to be insipid, but "tasty," or "tasteful," that is, "palatable," or acceptable, and perhaps even healing, since salt was one of three primary medicines in the Greco-Roman world. (Matthew records in 5:13 that Jesus says his disciples are to be "salt of the earth.") Salt may also be a reference to the thank offering of Exod 30:35 in which God commands Moses to "make an incense blended as by the perfumer, seasoned with salt, pure and holy." Gracious speech is speech that is pure and holy, and its purpose is to have answers for "everyone." "Answers for" not "arguments with."

Heretofore the parenesis in this section of the letter has suggested that, in so far as possible, the Colossians Christians live in ways that would be morally and ethically acceptable in their society. As noted, the vice and virtue lists, for example, have resonances in Greco-Roman teaching. However, the final phrase of verse six reminds us that the early Christians were subject to questioning (perhaps even legal cross examination) on the part of or by outsiders. As 1:13—2:23 suggest, the Colossian Christians may not only have to give answer to those outside their community, but to fellow believers who depart from the teaching they received from Epaphras as well as to those who are insisting on the necessity of "add ons" to their faith in Jesus Christ.

"Answer" suggests "respond to questions asked," not "start discussions or arguments." The imperative is not to be pugilistic and argumentative, which would draw exactly the kind of negative attention to the community that all of the author's parenesis in 3:5—4:6 wants to avoid. That this was a matter of great concern in the early church is borne out by references to similar concerns in 2 Tim 2:14-16 and 2:23-26 and Titus 3:2 and 9. No matter what polemics or verbal abuse the Christian encounters, she or he is to respond with grace, the principle attitude of God toward humanity which is manifested in the Lord Jesus Christ.

CONCLUSION

It is appropriate to allow 4:5-6, the author's summary *topoi* for the whole unit from 3:1 to 4:6, to serve as the conclusion of this chapter. The first instructional portion of his letter (1:13—2:4) focuses on christology. The second instructional portion, the hortatory material in 3:1—4:6 is, according to Lohse "equally determined by the theme of the universal dominion of Christ."[96] In the parenetic or teaching portion of the letter the implications of Christ's universal and cosmic dominion are worked out both in the individual's behavior and "in view of the various social positions in which individual members of the community live." Lohse continues "Just as there is the unfolding of the universal scope of the dominion of Christ in the first two chapters of the letter, the third and fourth chapters give an exposition of the ways in which the lordship of Christ includes all areas of our life."[97]

4

Paul's Associates in Colossians

(4:7–17)

INTRODUCTION

The apostle Paul is frequently, unjustly in my view, presented as thorny, argumentative, irascible, and misogynistic.[98] Certainly he held strong views strongly. This was because he understood how much was at stake for early Christian communities. But the careful reader of Paul finds him tender in his care for fellow workers (see, for example, Phil 2:19–25) and with a genius for friendship as the closing chapter of Romans and this section of the Colossian letter amply demonstrate. I have made the case elsewhere for a softening of our criticism of Paul's view of women.[99] While this chapter alludes to that matter, its focus is Paul's associates in ministry and his friends. Both categories include women.

Earlier chapters examined in some detail the structure of a Hellenistic letter, which generally concludes with wishes for good health to the recipients of the letter, the sending of greetings to others, and a peace wish.[100] Typical closings of Pauline letters are often introduced by or include hortatory remarks like those in Col 4:5–6, 10b, and 16, as well as greetings, the subject of this chapter. The peace wish is absent in the closing of Colossians, but was included in its standard opening formula, and ends with a grace and benediction (4:18) which we shall examine in the next chapter.

The main purpose of greetings in Hellenistic letters was emotional expression.[101] Greetings could be in first person, as the writer greeted someone; second person, as the writer asked the addressee to greet someone for him or her; or third person, as the writer relays a third party's greetings to the letter's recipients. The greetings themselves followed a clear grammatical form as follows: (1) A greeting verb is (2) followed by an indication of who is doing the greeting. (3) The person greeted is named, (4) followed by elaborating phrases which emphasize some aspect of the greeting.

The greeting of the Colossian letter follows these conventions and is unusually extensive. In a lecture at the École Biblique in Jerusalem in 1993, Jerome Murphy-O'Connor pointed out that Paul mentions individual persons only in letters he didn't found and in which he was generally not personally known. As in Romans 16, O'Connor thought that it is not necessary to assume that Paul (or in this case, the writer of Colossians) has met all the people mentioned, but he believes the point of these long greetings is precisely to establish relationships with those he hasn't met. As Lohse notes, "the long list of names clearly serves the purpose of establishing closer ties with the community."[102]

I think the case is slightly different in Colossae. Here, the people mentioned are either known to the writer and the church there, or are known to him and are being introduced to that church. The greeting falls into three sections. The first commends the messengers bringing the letter, the postmen (4:7–9). It then conveys greetings from the writer's fellow prisoners, and associated, the prisoners (4:10–14), and, finally, sends personal greetings and messengers to the writer's "pals" (4:15–17).

Since the theological and practical content of a Pauline letter is complete by the time one reaches the greeting, it would be easy to pass quickly over it. But the greetings give "flesh and blood" to Pauline epistles. Paul had real people around him for whom he cared and who cared for him. The greetings in the letters give insight into these friends and relationships within the church;

they show Paul's or an author's personal and pastoral concerns. Reconstructing those relationships through use of other Pauline, deutero-Pauline materials, and the Acts of the Apostles gives the author of Colossians a human face. While Pauline letters are generally accepted as containing the theological foundations of the church, the apostle, himself (and those who wrote in his name) is sometimes approached without sympathy. This is myopic and unfortunate because the authors of the Pauline letters had a genius for friendship and were accomplished pastors.

What follows presents the "human geography" of the Colossian letter, which, in part, increasingly dispose me to think it is Pauline.[103] I admit both that some of the following material is speculative in character and the caution with which I draw from its sources. I am not the first to do this sort of thing, and endeavors of this kind have been previously undertaken with varying degrees of scholarly rigor.[104]

THE POSTMEN (4:7-9)

The greeting of Colossians opens with the author's commendation of the carriers of the letter to the church at Colossae. The unit is framed by repetition of "will tell you" and "beloved brother" in v. 7 (*gnōrisei/agapētos adelphos*) and v. 9 (*agapētō adelphō/gnōrisousin*). It forms a neat compositional inclusion. The "brothers" (in Christ) Tychicus and Onesimus are entrusted with three tasks. First, they are to deliver the letter. "I have sent him" (*epempsa*, v. 8) uses an epistolary aorist, a way to attach a message in a letter that mentioned the carrier of the letter and suggested that he could fill out its contents with verbal reports. Second, Tychicus and Onesimus are to encourage (*parakalesē*, v. 8) the Colossians, in effect to serve as their "paracletes," those "called alongside" to help them. (We know that usage from John 14.) Finally, they are to share news of the author and his associates, "that you may know how we are," (v. 8) and "they will tell you about everything here" (v. 9).

Tychicus was a common name in inscriptions in Asia Minor. This Tychicus is called "beloved brother," meaning a beloved fellow

Christian, and "a faithful minister." He is also so designated in Eph 6:21 where he also serves as one who reports on that author's condition. "Minister" (*diakonos*) probably does not yet signify a clearly defined church office. Lohse notes the "'minister' . . . is not the holder of a fixed office in the community, but anyone who discharges a specific ministry."[105] Like Martha in Luke 11 (of whom the same root word is used), Tychicus is a servant of the church.

Tychicus is also the author's "fellow slave" (*syndoulos*, v. 7) in and of Christ.[106] Paul is fond of words compounded with *syn*. Such compounds either stress the apostle's union with Christ or his fellowship with other Christians, especially fellow "missionaries."[107] Acts 20:4 mentions a Tychicus from Asia who accompanied Paul through Macedonia. Paul apparently also send a Tychicus to Ephesus (2 Tim 4:12) and as a messenger to Crete. (Titus 3:12) If these references are to the same man, he served extensively as Paul's emissary. He apparently carried this letter to Colossae,[108] and his well known status as Paul's messenger would have served to commend Onesimus (even if the author of this letter were not Paul himself). In the absence of Paul, Tychicus and Onesimus "represented the apostolic heritage in the Lycus Valley."[109]

Onesimus was a common slave name and literally meant "useful one." There is no absolute proof that this is the same Onesimus who is the focus of the letter to Philemon, but that is the customary association since he is referred to as "one of you" (4:9).[110] Behind the mention of Onesimus is the whole issue of how slaves and masters were to be related to each other in the Christian community and household, a matter we examined in the household code in the previous chapter.[111] The Colossians must have been well aware of the specifics of this particular relationship, since Philemon 2 indicates that the letter discussing Onesimus and his master is to be read to the whole house church. Onesimus, too, is called "the faithful and beloved brother" (v. 9). Although full evaluation of Onesimus would require mastery of the substantial literature on slavery in the Greco-Roman world and the literature on the letter to Philemon, it appears that, already, the understanding of the relationship between slaves and free persons was being worked out very differently in the Christian communities of Asia Minor.[112]

Perhaps *unlike* the inaccurate teachers of concern to the writer of Colossians, Tychicus and Onesimus are "faithful," that is, committed to the apostolic (Pauline) message brought to Colossae by Epaphras and supported by the author of the letter. They come carrying this teaching with its apostolic authority to the Lycus Valley and are to be well received by the church in Colossae.

THE PRISONERS (4:10-14)

This longest section of the greeting conveys the greetings of the author's fellow prisoners and associates to those in the Colossian church (what Mullins' article calls "third person greetings"). These fellow prisoners and associates are named in two groups of three: Aristarchus, Mark, and Jesus-Justus; and Epaphras, Luke, and Demas. The first three, like the author, are Jews ("ones of the circumcision"[113]) and "a comfort to me" (v. 11).

Aristarchus is a "fellow prisoner," a *synaichmalōtos* (note the Pauline *syn-* prefix), a word which literally means a prisoner of war. It may be used figuratively here, or it may subtly reflect the idea of cosmic conflict alluded to in 1:13 and 2:15. It is certainly to be understood as an honorific title.[114] (And see 2 Cor 2:14 and 10:3-4.) The Acts of the Apostles introduces an Aristarchus, a native of Thessalonica who worked with Paul in Asia. He was among the crowd in the riot at Ephesus where he is referred to as a Macedonian and travel companion of Paul (Acts 19:29). He accompanied Paul (perhaps as a fellow prisoner?) through Macedonia (Acts 20:4) and on the ship to Italy (Acts 27:2). The letter to Philemon also names him as a fellow worker who sends greetings (Phlm 24). As one already associated with the area and known in proconsular Asia, if this is the same Aristarchus, the church would have had special reason to be concerned for him and to be pleased by news of him.

Mark is introduced parenthetically as a cousin of Barnabas, implying that he may not be as widely known as his cousin.

Apparently the Colossians are acquainted with Barnabas who thus provides Mark with legitimacy and who was willing to excuse his earlier lapses.[115] If this is the John Mark of Acts, the son of the Mary whose home in Jerusalem was a meeting place of Christians (Acts 12:12), his history as a missionary is fascinating. He was brought to Jerusalem by Barnabas and Paul after their early missions (Acts 12:25). He began the Cypriot mission with Paul, but left to return to Jerusalem (Acts 13: 5,13). Paul declined to take him with Barnabas on a visit to established churches, probably because of this earlier desertion, and this led to a rupture between Barnabas and Paul (Acts 15:36–41).

By the time of the writing of Colossians, it seems that Mark has been reinstated as a worker for the gospel and a companion of the author (Paul?). He, with the others in this trilogy is called a "fellow worker" (*synergoi,* v. 11, another use of *syn*), a term also applied to him in Phlm 24, and he also is a comfort to the author. The Colossians have "received instructions" about him, suggesting there has been some discussion of his work, and they are now to receive him, thus strengthening his position. In 2 Timothy, Mark seems fully to have regained his reputation and is described by that author both as *diakonos* and "as useful in my ministry (2 Tim 4:11). Also, in 1 Pet 5:13 a Mark adds his greetings to the "exiles of the dispersion" including those in Asia (1 Pet 1:1). It is therefore possible to read Mark's story as an example of how Christian workers can have a serious "falling out" or disagreement, and yet be reconciled and come to work together fruitfully again.

Little can be known of Jesus called Justus (v. 11). "Jesus" was a very common name in the period. "Justus," of course, means "the just." Double names were common among Jews who took Hellenistic names similar to their Semitic ones. (Recall John/Mark or Saul/Paul.) Jesus Justus, the only name in this threesome that does not also appear in Philemon, like Aristarchus and Mark is a "fellow worker"[116] and "of the circumcision." The latter phrase suggests they were Jews, but has also been interpreted to mean both Christians who were concerned with living a Jewish life style ("godfearers") and men of the circumcision party (perhaps like those in Galatia), although this second reading has not won wide acceptance. As Lohse notes, verse 11 alludes to the struggles the author of the letter (Paul?) faced with regard to the Law, conflicts that led some to abandon him.[117] These men have been a comfort to the author. *Paregoria*, used only here in the New Testament, implies comfort in its most profound sense. Derivatives of the word are found in medical contexts with the sense of "assuaging" or "alleviating," and the word has been found on gravestones and in a letter of condolence.[118] Do these men offer the author comfort in the face of what Paul in his prison epistles (or the author of this letter) understood to be impending death? (See Phil 1:12–26 and Col 4:18.) If that is the suggestion, it increases the persuasive intensity of the plea in this letter.

Turning to the second trio of names (Epaphras, Luke, and Demas), Epaphras may be as shortened form of Epaphroditus, and if that is the case, the man so named in Phil 2:25–30, though many scholars find this association tenuous. Like Onesimus, Epaphras is a Colossian whom the author here describes as "a servant of Christ Jesus." The word translated "servant" by the NRSV is actually "slave." Paul calls himself a "slave of Christ Jesus," but the only other of his associates so described is Timothy in Phil 1:1. Epaphras is a "fellow prisoner" of this letter's author who has brought the gospel to Colossae (1:7; 2:5) and who still bears responsibility for the Colossian church (and perhaps also for the churches in Laodicea and Heirapolis, about twelve miles from Colossae) through his prayers.

"Wrestling in his prayers" (v. 12) is an attempt to convey the sense of the Greek word *agōnizomenos* (note the root from which the English word "agony" derives), which is the same word used by Luke 22:44 to describe Jesus' prayer in the garden of Gethsemani. The author of this letter uses it to describe his own strivings for the gospel (1:29). The substance of Epaphras's prayer is similar to the author's in 1:3–12. Epaphras prays that the Colossians will be mature (*teleioi*) and fully assured (*peplērophoremenoi*)[119] in the will of God. The word contains the root *plērōma*, which has figured in the discussion of the inaccurate teachers and would be remembered by the letter's recipients. These two terms clearly allude to the rival claims mentioned earlier in the letter which Epaphras's prayer, like that of the author's, is intended to oppose.

The author's confidence in Epaphras and his commendation of him is certainly intended to inspire the Colossians' further confidence and trust in him. It has been noted that Paul's expression of confidence in those he addresses appears most frequently in the closings of letters and are intended to help secure a favorable hearing for his positions.[120] In praising Epaphras, the author (a consummate psychologist) is praising the Colossians since Epaphras is "one of you" (v. 12), and thus encouraging their faithfulness to his own understanding of the gospel.

Luke and Demas essentially are mentioned in passing. The Colossian letter is a primary source of the tradition of Luke the evangelist as Luke the "Beloved Physician." His separation from the men in vv. 10–11 indicate that he is a Gentile. A Luke is also mentioned in Phlm 24 as a fellow worker who sends greetings and in 2 Tim 4:10–11 as the only one who has remained with the Apostle Paul.[121] Demas (possibly an abridged form of Demetrius or Democritus or Demosthenes) seems also to be one of Paul's fellow workers and associates. In 2 Tim 4:10, however, one Demas " . . . in love with this present world, has deserted me and gone to Thessalonica." If Mark represents the happy fact of reconciliation of the estranged, Demas may represent the sad fact of rifts in fellowship in the Christian community even in its earliest days. He is the only person mentioned here in Colossians without commendation.

That Onesimus, Epaphras, Mark, Aristarchus, Demas, Luke, and Archippus also appear in Philemon further links the two letters and church communities. Those who argue for the pseudonymity of Colossians suggest these names are introduced to root the letter in the life of Paul. But it can equally be the case that they were, indeed, Paul's associates, as are Tychicus and Nympha who are not mentioned in Philemon and who are otherwise unknown.

THE PALS (4:15–17)

Having passed along the greetings of those attending him (second person greetings), the author now sends his own "first person" greetings. As is characteristic in the uncontested letters of Paul, the author uses a form of *aspazomai* (*aspasathe*, v. 15) to convey greetings. First, he greets "the brethren [*adelphous*] in Laodicea." This raises a thorny problem. Why would the author send greetings to Laodicea via Colossae if, as verse 16 asserts, he sent Laodicea a letter? The mention of a Laodicean letter which does not appear in our New Testament had led to much speculation. Among the theories are that the letter to Laodicea is the Ephesian letter (Marcion's suggestion), that it was a letter written by Epaphras,[122] and that it was written by the apostle Paul but later suppressed or lost, perhaps in the earthquake of AD 60/61 in the Lycus Valley. The historical puzzle remains, and the letter in question has not yet been accounted for.

In spite of the questions it raises, 4:15–16 offers significant information about the life of the early Pauline churches. First, it provides a tantalizing but incomplete suggestion of how the Pauline letters were collected. At an early stage they were apparently exchanged among the churches and later collated. Second, it is apparent from 1:24–2:5 that the author intended (as did Paul) that his letters be read aloud in the churches, and 4:16 makes this explicit (compare 1 Thess 5:27 and Phlm 2) Third, these verses reinforce the fact that Christians met together in homes in smaller groups and that the groups had fellowship with each other. There is ample New Testament evidence elsewhere for such house churches (see Acts 16:15, 40 and Rom 16:5, 23). Abraham J. Malherbe's *Social Aspects of Early Christianity* provides an engaging and accessible look "inside" the house churches.[123]

Some of the Pauline house churches were clearly headed by women. Nympha, like Mary (Acts 12:12) and Lydia (Acts 16:11–15, 40), seems to have been a householder who provided one of the churches in the Colossian area with a place to meet. Textual matters have raised questions about whether "Nympha" is a male or a female name. Some scholars suggest it is a short form of Nymphodorus, noting, however, that the contracted form in rare.[124] While it is true that Nympha appears as a woman's name in Latin inscriptions and has been found as a woman's name in Greek literature,[125] textual evidence is divided on whether the pronoun in the following phrase is *autēs* (feminine) or *autou* (masculine).

In his 1882 commentary, Lightfoot makes an interesting remark. "Of these alternative readings . . . *autou* is condemned by its simplicity, and *autes* has arisen from the form *Numphan*, which *prima facie* would look like a woman's name, and yet hardly can be so."[126] But why not? Because the feminine form is unusual? Because a woman could not be the leader of a house church? There are several clear examples in the New Testament of women who headed house churches: Chloe in Corinth of whom Paul knows and apparently approves (1 Cor 1:11) or Dorcas or Lydia in Acts. This latter was Schweizer's explanation of the issue. He suggests that perhaps "an original 'her' was subsequently changed to 'his,' because at a later stage it could not be conceived of that a woman might be responsible for an entire house community."[127]

The change to the masculine pronoun and interpretation does seem to have happened in the course of the transmission of the text.[128] Bernadette Brooten has demonstrated that this same "sex change" happened to Junia in Rom 16:7.[129] Although the textual problem has not been definitively resolved, it is my opinion that Nympha is another example of the prominence of women in the early church generally, and in the Pauline churches in particular. (I have argued elsewhere that the prominence of women in earliest Christianity caused difficulties which led to their being suppressed later.[130] Like Lydia, Nympha was head of her own household (we can safely assume this since no male is mentioned in connection with her) which may have included children, relatives, and slaves. (see 3:18—4:1). As such, Nympha was a businesswoman of sorts since she would have been responsible to manage the affairs of this household.[131]

Finally, the author of Colossians reminds Archippus to be faithful to the ministry he received in the Lord. Archippus is mentioned in Philemon 2 as a member of Philemon's household and a "fellow soldier" (*synstratiotes*, literally "with-fighter") of Paul. John Knox has argued that it was Archippus who owned Onesimus. The verse in Colossians, he asserts, is to remind him of what he had been instructed in Philemon.[132] Whether or not this is so is (like many things in the Colossian letter) debatable.[133] Abbott thinks Archippus was probably a son of Philemon and a presbyter or evangelist in Colossae.[134]

Verse 17 tantalizes modern readers but does not reveal much that is uncontested. Is Archippus to be faithful to his ministry generally, or to some specific task to which the writer of Colossians has called him? Is the verse a warning or a positive reminder? Is "received in the Lord" (*parelabes en kyriō*) technical language, so that v. 17 reflects, as v. 7 does not, the beginning of a an order like the diaconate? Like the recipient of Philemon, Archippus will be given his instructions from the letter's writer at a public meeting of the church. Whatever it is he is to do will be known and expected by the community. The message and the circumstances of its delivery are calculated to impress Archippus with the solemnity of his responsibility[135] and to ensure he will carry it out. As Paul did on Philemon, the author of Colossians has placed not so subtle pressure on Archippus and the accomplishment of his ministry.

CONCLUSION

As Lohse has pointed out, these messages and greetings serve the author of Colossians first, as proof of an apostolic message, and, second, as recommendation of those named to the Christian community at Colossae (and Laodicea) as faithful ministers and helpers of the writer.[136] But who were Tychicus, Onesimus, Aristarchus, Mark, Jesus-Justice, Epaphras, Luke, Demas, Nympha, and Archippus? We know very little about them. Most of what we can reconstruct is speculative.

I think these names represent people who are living examples of a genius for friendship and the pastoral nature of the writer of the letter. They undercut a stereotype of Paul (if he is the author) as a thorny and unlikeable, pious dictator. The reveal a pastor who had as his primary concern the eternal destiny of those about whom he cared and to whom he entrusted "the word of truth" (1:5).

5

The Spirituality of the Colossian Letter

". . . we have not ceased praying for you . . ." (1:2a, 3–12; 4:2–4, 18)

". . . Christ in you . . ." and ". . . hid with Christ in God . . ." (1:27; 2:6–7; 3:1–4; 4:2–6)

INTRODUCTION

This book opened with a series of "what if" questions: What if Paul were *not* viewed as a rather pugilistic and argumentative theologian, but as a spiritual master? What if the Church had presented him not so much as a shaper of Christian doctrine and ecclesial practice, but as a person of remarkably wide experience of and wisdom in the life of prayer, say as a really wise spiritual director? What if the Pauline letters were read primarily as spiritual documents? And what if we read Colossians that way? That's exactly what we'll do in this final chapter by looking first at the written or vocalized prayers in Colossians and then, very briefly, at the mysterious and beautiful "in Christ" language that is at the heart of the author's understanding of what it means to be a Christian.

I have come to think of the Pauline epistles as prayer documents. In fact, judged by literary form, the template which Paul used in writing to the churches, the Hellenistic letter, is shaped as a prayer document. The format of Paul's letters is well known.[137] In miniature, that form is very clear in Philemon. (The verses in parentheses in what follows in this paragraph refer to that letter.) An opening formula including the sender, addressee and an opening greeting/grace wish (vv. 1–3) is followed by a thanksgiving prayer which sets forth the theme of the letter and reveals Paul's attitude toward its recipients (vv. 4–5, 6–7). Only Galatians and 2 Corinthians lack this thanksgiving, supposedly because Paul is too annoyed with those communities to be thankful. (To be spiritual does not mean to be passionless! Quite the opposite in fact.) The body or "meat" of a Pauline letter often follows the order theory/ praxis, that is, the theological or theoretical material is followed by parenesis, practical advice and exhortation, and often concludes with Paul's travel plans. Since most of his contemporaries heard rather than read Paul's letters (and even private reading was aloud), the travel plans serve as the auditory clue that the letter is concluding (vv. 8–21, 22). The closing formula includes hortatory remarks, a peace wish, greetings, and a grace wish or benediction (vv. 23–24).

As a brief aside, while we are considering Philemon, I remind you that Timothy is also its co-author, that both of the authors are in prison, that the slave Onesimus whose situation led to the letter is probably the same Onesimus we met in Col 4:9, and that several names of people addressed or greeted appear in both letters suggesting ties between Philemon's community and that of the Colossians.

My point in rehearsing the Pauline letter format is that whatever is treated in the body of a Pauline letter (which can also contain reports of prayer, prayer wishes, doxologies, and teachings on prayer) is framed by prayer in the opening and closing grace or benediction and is introduced by a prayer of thanksgiving and intercession. What follows will briefly consider the opening and closing benedictions of Colossians (1:2b and 4:18), its opening thanksgiving and prayer (1:3–12), and the prayer *topoi* in 4:2–4.

Before we turn to that material, a lexical note is in order. There are four uses of the word "prayer" in Colossians. Three are forms of the verb *proseuchomai,* which means "to offer prayer" or simply "to pray." In 1:3, 9, and 4:3 the form is *proseuchomenoi,* a present middle participle. "The present tense points to a repeated action."[138] In 4:2 the basic noun root word *proseuche* is used, which in Hellenistic Greek meant "prayer addressed to God" and had the derived meaning of a place set apart for prayer. (See Acts 16:13 for this usage.) In classical Greek it could mean a vow, a wish, or an aspiration. While there are a range of words for prayer in the New Testament, this is the most common.[139]

OPENING AND CLOSING BENEDICTORY FORMULAE

Opening Formula (1:2b)

The opening blessings in Paul's letters exhibit great uniformity. "Grace and peace from God our Father and the Lord Jesus Christ" is the usual form. Paul never uses the secular greeting *salus* perhaps because what he invokes for the letter's recipients are theological blessings. In a very interesting article, Van Elderen suggests that the salutation functions like the invocation in worship. The verb is normally in the optative which, more than mere volition, suggests the speaker's confidence of fulfillment.[140] Paul asks knowing that what he asks for will be fulfilled because of whom he asks it.

It is worth remembering that in the biblical tradition, and in Paul's day (unlike our own), language was understood to be powerful. Blessings and curses were power-laden words. In blessing there was power inherent in the words themselves. As a "Hebrew born of Hebrews" (Phil 3:5), Paul knew that Hebrew Scripture contained two major forms of blessings: pronouncements *of* blessing and petitions *for* blessing. YHWH was understood as the source of all blessing, and God's people were instructed to seek his blessings. Because God's blessing found expression in his people's history, people could be confident about asking for future blessings on the basis of those they had been granted in the past.[141] Certainly the "Jesus Jews" whom the author addressed in Colossae would have shared his understanding.

Like many of the openings in Paul's letters, the one in Colossians alludes to the author's authority ("apostle . . . by the will of God"), introduces a co-author, ("Timothy") and indicates his relationship to the recipients, "saints and faithful brothers." A better translation of *adelphois* would be "faithful ones" or "faithful brethren." Jerry Sumney notes that "no other letter in the Pauline corpus uses the term "brothers" as an address of the recipients."[142] I wonder whether Colossians' author is addressing *only* the *faithful* (*pistois*) brethren, but not those straying from Epaphras' teaching. In her commentary, Margaret MacDonald notes that the opening of Colossians indicates what was explored in chapter 4, that "Paul's ministry is a collaborative effort involving a network of relationships. This is suggested by the familial language in vv. 1–2 . . ."[143]

To this branch of the family of believers whom he has not met the author offers the blessings of grace and of peace, language which appears in Jewish letters of the period. (See, for example, 1 Maccabees 1:1.) In all of Paul's letters with the exception of 1 Thessalonians and Colossians, God and the Lord Jesus Christ are the source of the blessing. Perhaps the omission of "Jesus Christ" in Colossians' opening blessing is because the whole letter, and certainly the first chapters, focus on Christ. As suggested earlier, the letter to Colossians is written to correct a deficient christology.

Closing (or Benediction) Formula (4:18)

As a Pauline letter comes to a close, one usually finds some combination of hortatory remarks (in a form we earlier designated *topoi*), greetings to associates, and a wish of peace and grace, a benediction or blessing which picks up the grace wish from the opening formula. Grace and peace often form an inclusion around the body of Paul's letter. David Stanley, SJ argues convincingly that Paul has appropriated the formulae with which early Christian worship began and ended.[144] (It still does in liturgical traditions of Christianity, although in many Protestant traditions what is in fact a "charge" has eclipsed the more theological blessing form.) Similarly, Robert Jewett postulated a form in Pauline benedictions deriving from homiletical use with its lively sense of imparting divine blessings in early Christian preaching.[145] Early Christian preachers understood their words to be the conduits of God's blessing.

The author brings Colossians to a close with a "postscript" including his own autograph or signature, here asserting Paul's authorship (see also 1 Cor 16:21; Gal 6:11; 2 Thess 3:17). The author refers to his imprisonment which first appeared *not* in the discussion of his sufferings (1:24—2:5), but in the closing greetings from the author's co-workers to the Colossians (4:10). The author opened the letter by establishing his authority to speak to a congregation he hadn't met on the basis of a fact of Paul's biography: that God made Paul an apostle ("by the will of God," 1:1). He closes it with another mark of authority: his imprisonment for the Gospel which also exerts a certain emotional pressure on the Colossians to attend to his teaching. Reminder of his imprisonment was an emotional blackmail that the apostle Paul was not above using (see Phil 1:12–26 and 4:11–20). "Grace be with you" is a basic benedictory formula. It is usually specified as that of the Lord Jesus, but again, the Name is perhaps omitted here (as it is in the Pastoral Epistles) because the author thought it unnecessary after the extensive teaching about Jesus Christ in this letter which is bracketed by blessings for the Colossian Christians.

THE AUTHOR AT PRAYER:
THE THANKSGIVING AND PRAYER (1:3-12)

The "thanksgiving" of a Pauline letter actually includes two things: first, a thanksgiving for what Paul knows of the community (here 1:3–8) followed by, second, his prayer of petition for the community (here 1:9–12). Together they serve as a formal introduction to what follows in the body of the letter, and, read carefully, introduce the themes of the letter and Paul's attitude toward its recipients. Rhetorically it serves to "warm up the audience" and to secure their good will before the matter at hand is introduced. This was especially important when the "matter at hand" is Paul's dissatisfaction with a church or when he had not founded the church or met it's members.

Not surprisingly, thanksgivings begin *eucharisto to theo* (I give thanks) or in the plural, "we give thanks." Secular Greek letters from the period open "I give thanks to the gods" and also offer a prayer for the well-being of the recipients. They follow the form: verb of thanksgiving, modifier, object of thanksgiving, person or persons addressed, and substance of the thanksgiving.[146] Paul employs this form in one of two ways. "I give thanks to God" is followed by participial phrases explaining why, or it is followed by causal "because" (*hoti*) clauses. Within that general structural pattern one finds at least three types of material: 1. reports of thanksgiving by Paul; 2. petitionary prayer reports or "prayer wishes;" and 3. personal, apostolic details.[147]

Thanksgiving (1:3–8)

The thanksgiving in Col 1:3–8 details the author's reasons for thanks (vv. 3–6) and praises Epaphras (vv. 7–8). In Greek, the thanksgiving comprises one sentence, the first example of the long, grammatically complicated sentences that characterize the style of this and other late "Pauline" letters. The author thanks God and for the second time refers to God as "Father" (1:2, 3), this time of "our Lord Jesus Christ," expressing gratitude for the theological virtues of the Colossian Christians: their *faith* in Christ Jesus, *love* for all the saints, and the *hope* "laid up for you in heaven" (vv. 4–5). Sumney points out that these "three elements appear together nowhere in the new Testament outside the Pauline corpus."[148] That hope is "stored" for them in heaven suggests is it a gift, not self-generated. Perhaps the Colossian Christians are to remember this when told they must do or not do certain things. Christianity is a gift received before it is an action required.

The locus of this hope is "the word of truth, the gospel" (v. 5), again, perhaps a gentle allusion to alternative teachings in 2:8–23 which are not true. "Truth" (*alētheia*) connotes God's will and word in Pauline texts like Rom 2:8 and Gal 2:5. Just as Jesus taught that "you will know them by their fruits" (Matt 7:16–20), here the truth of a teaching is authenticated by the growth it elicits. And it is worth noting that one criteria of "truth" in the Greco-Roman world was that a teacher followed or lived by his own teaching. The biographical material in Colossians is intended to suggest its author does so. The gospel (not the Colossian Christians) is what is "bearing fruit and growing" throughout the Roman Empire even as it has among them. The author has heard good things of them (v. 4), and they have heard the gospel (v. 6) from Epaphras who has reported their response to the author who has heard of it and now responds.

"Just as," forms of *kathos* (not so evident in English translations) are repeated three times in vv. 6 and 7 to link the success of the gospel in the Empire and among the Colossian Christians with what they have heard from Epaphras whom the author praises as "a beloved fellow slave" (*syndoulou*) and "faithful (*pistos*) minister of Christ" (vv. 7–8). The compound *syndoulou* appears only in Colossians and depicts leaders in the Christian community as slaves of God, not themselves authoritarian, but completely at the bidding of another. (Recall in this context 3:22—4:1 on slaves and masters.) It invites the Colossians "to envision a type of leadership that is consistent with the gospel rather than with cultural expectations."[149] (One cannot help recalling that this reflects the alternative form of leadership Jesus envisages in Mark 10:43–45.) Associating himself with their evangelist, Epaphras, who has reported good things about the community gives the author a connection to and license to write to the Colossian Christians. Indeed, it is the Colossians' love reported by Epaphras to the author that leads him to pray for the community.

P. T. O'Brien points out that the Pauline thanksgivings are linked to the Gospel itself, for its right reception by the recipients of letters. The Gospel is viewed as dynamic; according to Sumney, it has power, is "regarded as a living force." O'Brien notes, "Paul's prayers of thanksgiving are directed to God in gratitude for what he [God] has done through the gospel. He [the author] . . . looks with confidence to a similar dynamic activity in the lives of believers themselves."[150]

Prayer/Intercession (1:9–12)

In my view 1:9–12 is the prayer proper, and 1:13–14 provides the transition to the Christ hymn. The prayer in 1:9–12 has many parallels with the thanksgiving: both speak of constant prayer for the recipients; both use the phrases "from the time we heard" and "bearing fruit and growing;" both speak of knowing, giving thanks, a possession in heaven, "the Father," and both use "all" repeatedly. O'Brien has noted that the interrelation of the thanksgiving and petition is "more marked in the Colossian prayer than anywhere else" and exhibits greater emphasis on knowledge than in any other Pauline petition because correct knowledge leads to proper conduct.[151] And, of course, it is correct knowledge of Christ that will address and solve the Colossian church's difficulty.

But while vv. 3–8 describe strengths of the community, vv. 9–11 address their spiritual needs. In a complex series of participial phrases (many of which are in the passive voice suggesting these are things that will be given by God, not things they must do or achieve themselves, an important point in light of 2:6–23) the author prays that they will be filled (a form of *pleroma* discussed earlier) with knowledge of God's will, spiritual wisdom and understanding, in order that they may lead lives worthy of and pleasing to the Lord, that is, by bearing fruit and growing in knowledge of God. The author prays they will be made strong with God's strength and prepared to endure, an allusion to possible persecution, since *hypomone* "means fortitude and perseverance especially in relation to an external threat."[152]

The petitions of vv. 9–11 move toward thanksgiving in vv. 12–14 for what God has *already* done. As suggested earlier, this is exactly how petitionary prayer works: on the basis of what

God has accomplished for one in the past, one dares to ask for future blessings. In fact, Margaret MacDonald calls the author's strategy for responding to the Colossian situation "a strategy of remembrance."[153] The verbs describing God's activity are strong. God has enabled (*ikanoō*, "made sufficient" or "qualified"), rescued (*ruomai* "delivered"), and transferred (*methistēmi* "delivered" or "transferred" as in moving to form a new colony). The writer suggests that God is active and present, has enabled the Colossian Christians to share the inheritance of the saints in light, not because of anything they have done or experienced, but because of divine activity, indeed, divine grace. God's fatherhood was alluded to twice at the letter's outset. Together with the language of inheritance this would have extremely strong resonances because in the Greco-Roman world, the father determined who would receive inheritance.[154]

Finally, then, the image of light at the end of v. 12 provides the transition to vv. 13–14 which move seamlessly from the prayer to the Christ hymn (and, of course, hymns are sung prayers), the passage of central importance to all the teaching in the letter. God who has given the Colossians the inheritance of the saints in light, has also rescued them from "the power of darkness," another powerful image several commentators suggest is a circumlocution for "Satan." (And recall John 1:5.) Verses 13–14 summarize God's saving acts and, according to MacDonald, "might be viewed as a . . . succinct statement of a sentiment that runs from 1:1—2:7."[155]

THE AUTHOR'S TEACHING ON PRAYER
(4:2–4)

When we looked at the author's teaching in the parenetic sections of the letter, we noted how the *topoi* of 3:15–17 and 4:2–6 frame the household code in 3:18—4:1. We might think of the teaching in 3:15–17 to inculcate attitudes of prayerfulness (rootedness in Christ and in gratitude) and 4:2–4 to address some of the "how-tos of prayer." Indeed, Pauline letters frequently close with *topoi* on prayer (see Rom 15:30–31; Eph 6:18–20; Phil 4:4–7;

1 Thess 5:16–19, 25). As the author has "not ceased praying for [them]" (1:9), so the Colossians are to "devote" (from the root verb *proskaptereō*, "to adhere to" or "busy oneself with") themselves to prayer.

Sumney points out that "this continuous prayer does not consist of requests for particular needs, but the act of being in the presence of God, offering praise and thanksgiving." "Such access to God assumes that believers do not need the spiritual experiences that the visionaries offer because they already have access to God."[156] Herein is one of the most hidden and helpful definitions of prayer in the New Testament: to be prayerful is to be awake and alert, aware of being constantly in God's presence.

"Keeping alert it in" is a very potent phrase in part because *grēgorountes* ("be alert" or "watch") is the very verb the evangelist Mark ascribes to Jesus in desperate circumstances in the Garden of Gethsemane and what he charges his disciples to do especially in times of tribulation. (See Mark 13:34–25, 37; 14:35, 37–38.) The idea is of keeping alert *by means of* prayer. Prayer is what keeps spiritual vision acute. That prayer is a source of clear vision is especially important in the context of discernment about various teachings. "With thanksgiving" is a leitmotiv that echoes through the spirituality of Colossians like a theme in a Wagnerian opera (see, for example, 1:3, 12; 2:7; 3:15, 16, 17).

Requests for prayer are common in Pauline letters. This author is humble enough to ask people to pray for him. Here the request is "pray for *us*," (italics mine) presumably the author, his co-author Timothy, and those with them in prison, and is not so much for them personally as for the success of their mission. The Colossians are asked to pray that God "will open to us a door for the word" (an ironic turn of phrase for a collection of jail birds!) in order that they may declare "the mystery of Christ" (a phrase previously used in 1:26, 27; and 2:2–3) "for which I am in prison." In the ancient world, the metaphor of the open door signified freedom to act or live as one desired.[157] The phrase is *di' 'ho kai dedemai*, "for which I also have been bound, or chained." The author is asking for prayers that he continue to do precisely what he did that has landed him in prison. He wants them to pray that he "may reveal it clearly." "Reveal" (*phaneroso*, "make manifest") is the language of the mystery religions. As Paul does in other letters, here the author is apparently using the language of the upstart teachers to subvert their position. The author of Ephesians, with which Colossians is so closely linked, certainly does this.

Paul, if he is the author of Colossians, or its author, regards prayer as one of the supremely important functions of his apostolic commission. He commends Epaphras for it in 4:12. The author's prayer is habitually focused on his apostolic work.[158] By means of his lexical choices in these three verses, the author recapitulates the great themes of the epistle: the centrality of thanksgiving, the mystery of Christ, his own circumstances, and the need for clear and accurate teaching. And he has set forth several general principles of prayer as follows:

1. The Christian should be "devoted to it," engage in it frequently.

2. "Keeping alert in it" suggests both vigilant prayer and that prayer, itself, clarifies one's vision.

3. Prayer should always include thanksgiving. As Br. David Steindl Rast teaches gratitude is "the heart of prayer."[159]

4. It is appropriate for a Christian to solicit the prayers of others for himself/herself.

5. The Christian's prayer should focus on the great mission of the Church which is the mystery of Christ, the radiant reality that shines through the whole epistle and the whole universe and to which we now turn.

IN CHRIST AND CHRIST WITHIN

What we've examined thus far are primarily literary prayer forms, formal aspects of a Greco-Roman letter that are, in fact patterns for prayer, models or methods of prayer, if you will. I don't want to diminish the importance of this fact in interpreting Colossians, or any other letter in the Pauline corpus. Not understanding Pauline letters in the light of the fact that they are framed by prayer and contain many prayer forms, prayers, and teachings on prayer has led to their interpretation and use of those letters in some very peculiar ways and to rather serious misunderstanding of Paul, himself. At the same time it is true, as Ruth Burrows, OCD points out in her book *The Essence of Prayer,* "Methods are not Prayer" and "the heart of prayer [is] to remain open to the inflowing of divine love."[160] Prayer is something God does or, if we believe Colossians, God *is* in the believer.[161] A form of prayer can be the opening to God whose face, or *ikon* to use the letter's own term, in the Colossian letter is that of the Christ. To use a phrase from the letter, in Colossians "Christ is all and in all" (3:13). Christians are in Christ, and Christ is in them.

The text of Colossians suggests that in this vibrant Christian community, there existed a lack of understanding of the completeness of Christ. Not unlike the "spirituals" or "charismatics" in the Corinthian church, the Colossian Christians didn't yet glimpse the encompassing meaning of Christ. So the subject of the letter to the Colossians *is* Christ.[162] It is an early Christian document which focuses on christology and the effect or consequences of Christ and baptism into Christ both in cosmic and personal contexts. The two theological centers of the letter explain his cosmic importance in 1:15–20 and its personal implications for the baptized in 1:21–23 and 2:6–15, and by extension, 3:1—4:6 which is introduced by five references to Christ in four verses. Christ is not only the image, but the fullness of God (1:15, 19; 2:9).

Full stop. Take that in for a moment. It means that Christ was pre-eminent, existing even before the beginning of creation, from whom it all came (1:15, 16) and in whom it all coheres (1:17). Thus far we have a wisdom theology and, parenthetically, one echoed in the great opening hymn of John's gospel. If Colossians is written after Paul's death, it would indeed be closer to the time of the writing of John. This, alone, was a critical teaching in an environment of cultural and religious pluralism (probably Asia Minor). But Colossians goes farther, asserting that by means of Christ, God reconciles everything to God:[163] "through him God was pleased to reconcile to himself *all things*, whether on earth or in heaven, by making peace through the blood of his cross" (1:20, italics mine, and 2: 13–14). N.T. Wright suggests that God's purpose in creation was to sum up all things in Jesus Christ.[164] (Often to their confusion, I used to tell my seminary students that the reason for creation was resurrection.) Colossians reminds those Christians and us that we can't think too expansively about Jesus Christ. There is nothing in creation in which we cannot find Christ. To quote the Holy Qu'ran "Where so ere ye look there is the face of God" (Sura 2:115).

The great paradox of the Colossian letter which should inform any truly Christian spirituality is that the all-encompassing immensity of Christ in which Christians dwell, also *dwells in us*. In an apparent geographical or spatial conundrum, Colossians proclaims a bi-locational mystery. First, "God's mystery . . . is Christ himself, in whom are hidden all the treasures of wisdom and knowledge" (2:2–3). The Colossians don't have to look elsewhere or add on anything to their faith in Christ; he is everywhere, at all times, and in every way perfection. And by their baptism into Christ "you have died, and *your life is hidden with Christ in God*" (3:3, italics mine). Christ is the environment, the milieu in which the Christian dwells. "You have received Christ Jesus the Lord," the writer of Colossians says and so commands, "live your lives in him, rooted and built up in him . . ." (2:6–7). God isn't somewhere else. The baptized "live and move and have their being" in Christ/God (to quote Paul quoting Greek philosophy to the Athenians in Acts 17: 28).

That extraordinary truth is half of the conundrum. The second half is the Colossian letter's assertion that "God chose to make known how great among the Gentiles are the riches of the glory of this mystery, which is *Christ in you*, the hope of glory" (1:27, italics mine). The One in whom "the whole fullness of deity dwells bodily," the one in whom "you have come to fullness" (2:9–10) *indwells* you. The Word has not only become flesh and *lived* (dwelt) among us (John 1:14), it has taken up residence *within* us.

There is another reason, not to my knowledge heretofore noted, why the concept of "Christ within" would have had particularly powerful resonances in Colossae, in Asia Minor, and in general in the Greco-Roman religious world. Recall that in the Semitic world the gods were geographic. There were the gods of Philistia or of Babylon, for example. The God of the Israelites was different in that YHWH was understood at least by one strain of thought as a God of a people and of time (history), not of place. In the book of Exodus, for example, God travelled with the people. Although a Temple for God was built in Jerusalem during the United Monarchy, this concept that God was not bound to geography was in part what allowed the religion to survive exile in Babylon. When the people were carried away from Jerusalem and the Temple where God "resided" in the Holy of Holies, God's provident care for them did not end. Fast forward to AD 70 and the destruction of the Second Temple in Jerusalem, the one built after the return from Babylon. One of the many traumas of the time of the Roman destruction of Jerusalem for both Jews and "Jesus Jews" or Christians was the question of whether God was still *with* them. The Colossian letter says to Jewish Christians, "Yes. God is with you and *within* you."

The Colossian church and the letter to it probably date from the 60s. The Christians in Colossae who had been Jews already had experience of God as "with them" regardless of place (although the destruction of the Temple in Jerusalem as a symbol must have been a shock when it happened). What of the Gentile Christians? In the Greco-Roman world, the gods were worshipped in temples in which the statue of the deity represented (or *was*) its presence. An example from Asia Minor will make the point for Colossae.

The temple of Artemis in Ephesus was, relatively speaking, not geographically far from Colossae. Artemis (Roman Diana) was widely worshipped in the ancient world as a mother goddess who looked after nature and fertility. (She was also known as Cybele, Atargatis, and Ashtoreth). Her original temple in Ephesus, some 375 by 180 feet in area with 60-foot-tall marble columns was completed about 500 BC. She was so revered that, when that first temple was destroyed by Alexander the Great, it was rebuilt, completed about 250 BC and was one of the Seven Wonders of the World at the time. Her statue portrays her with multiple breasts (or perhaps eggs, archaeologists differ, but both are symbols of fertility and life giving) and a skirt decorated with bands of animals and birds. It is supposition on my part, but not unrealistic to think that among the Colossians Christians were those who had worshipped Ephesian Artemis.

The Acts of the Apostles 19 is set in Ephesus, where Paul teaches, and God performs miracles through him. Acts 19:23–41 deals with a disturbance in which the silversmiths "who made silver shrines of Artemis" (Acts 19:24) were disgruntled because "this Paul has persuaded and drawn away a considerable number of people by saying that gods made with hands are not gods." The silversmiths were upset because their trade was being diminished by Christian evangelism, and they feared that "the temple of the great goddess Artemis will be scorned, and she will be deprived of her majesty that brought all Asia and the world to worship her" (24: 26–27).

Acts 19:21–41 is an engaging account of religions in tension, and one that provides a great deal of information about how Greco-Romans worshipped and thought about their gods. But the point for our study of Colossians is that Gentile Colossians would have been accustomed to going to a temple to worship with the god's statue. But Jesus Christ had no temple. (Special buildings set aside for Christian worship are apparently not earlier than the third century AD.) So, where was the Christ? Where do we worship him? These would have been legitimate questions. The answer to both is "within you." Paul, whose missions to the gentiles would have faced exactly the problem we are considering, used the language of the believer's body as a temple in 1 Cor 3:16–17 and 2 Cor 6:16 in which he asserts "we are the temple of the living God." The Gentile believer in Christ Jesus had no need for a temple because he or she *was* the temple within which Christ dwelt. This idea is part of what stands behind the author's explanation to the Colossians of "the mystery that has been hidden . . . but has now been revealed to his saints . . ." The mystery is "Christ in you, the hope of glory" (1:26–27). That Christ is within the believer solved a practical problem for new Christians from non-Jewish backgrounds, and invites all Christians to an interiority that understands a mystical reality. Christ is both the "environment" in which they "live and move and have their being" (Acts 17:28, as per Paul's Areopagus speech to the Athenians) and indwells the believer.

If the Christian's spiritual practices are solely a matter of using prayer forms verbally to address God "out there somewhere" (4:2), or of thinking it is necessary to engage in dietary observances (3:16) or liturgical festivals (3:16) or asceticism (3:21) or "self-imposed piety. . .and severe treatment of the body" (3:23), it may be the result of an underdeveloped or stunted christology. One's Christ might be too small, or, more darkly, he or she might be attempting to tame Christ's glorious wildness or win Christ's already given love. We Christian teachers have not done a very good job of teaching Christ's good people that He dwells within us with all that implies. How could He not? We receive him at baptism. We take Him into ourselves at the Eucharist.

What we have in Colossians is not only a nascent stage in the Church's early christology, but its understanding of the Trinity as well. In a fascinating, transcribed conversation between Benedictines David-Steindl-Rast and Anselm Grun, I was particularly taken by the section on the Trinity. There Anselm Grun suggests that "Trinity means the different ways in which God is in relationship with us, and we are in relationship with God: The God who is *outside* and different, the God who is *with us*, and the God who *permeates* us."[165] (Italics mine.) Although Colossians is not mentioned, this understanding of the Trinity goes a long way toward explaining its "geographical conundrum" that is how one might be both "in Christ" and have "Christ within." David Steindl-Rast uses the equally helpful image of "a vessel that is completely full of seawater and submerged in the sea."[166]

Finally, then, Christian spirituality in both the Eastern and Western church is manifested in a great many beautiful and fruitful external actions. I could be wrong, but it seems to me, we are not so good at attending to Christ *in us*, the hope of glory (1:27) and the consequences of that reality so clearly articulated in the Colossian letter. Ruth Burrows reminded us that a prayer form (or, in the terms of this letter, let us say, any consciously chosen external, spiritually motivated activity) can be the opening to God within. By means of them, she suggests "all we are trying to do is help ourselves to be present for God to love us."[167] The great and subtle spiritual gift of the Colossian letter is to remind us that, in Christ, God is ubiquitous, and, thus logically, of course, within us. "Within" is pretty close by. I am greatly taken by the Qur'anic teaching that God is as close as our jugular vein. "We [God] are nearer to him [human beings] than his jugular vein" (55:26–27). Perhaps if we shut up occasionally, felt in our own the Divine heartbeat, and listened within we would hear the "still, small voice" saying, "I love you." And that would change everything.

PART TWO

6

"We Have not Ceased Praying for You"

(1:1–14)

TEXTUAL NOTES

These verses reflect the standard opening of a Pauline letter. Verses 1 and 2 provide the names of the authors, the recipients of the letter, and express a "grace wish" which might be thought of as an opening blessing. The phrase "by the will of God" (v. 1) is a subtle allusion to the author's (Paul's?) authority as one called by God. That the letter is addressed to the "faithful brethren" (*pistois adelphois*) may hint that some in the Colossian community aren't faithful.

Verses 3–12 comprise the opening prayer. Verses 3–6 thank God that the Colossians exhibit the three cardinal Christian virtues: faith (in Christ), love (of the saints), and hope (of heaven). It contrasts what the author has heard of them (v. 4) with what they, themselves, have heard, the truth of the gospel (v. 5). Verses 7–8 introduce and commend Epaphras ("faithful minister") and his work among them. Already we have read two allusions to the sources of authority and two to "truth" which is proved by fruitfulness and growth.

Intercession follows thanksgiving. Verses 9–12a are the author's prayer for the community: that they will be filled with knowledge of God's will so that they may lead lives worthy of the Lord and pleasing. They are to bear fruit in good works (practical) and grow in knowledge of God (theological or spiritual). The author prays that they may be strong (the source of their strength being God's power) in order to endure (suggesting trial or persecution) and joyfully to give thanks to the Father.

Verses 12b–14 describe with particularly strong verbs what God has done for them: *enabled* their inheritance (an idea that will be revisited in the letter) with the saints, *rescued* them from the power of darkness, and *transferred* them to the kingdom of the Son, the source of their redemption. That the verbs are passive in the Greek underscore that the action is God's. The verses move the reader seamlessly from prayer to the Christ hymn, the central element in the letter and the answer to the difficulties in the Colossian church.

REFLECTION ON THE PASSAGE

How do you pray for people you don't know? It's an interesting question, isn't it? Honestly, I expect we don't do as much praying for those we don't know as we might. Our prayers are taken up with intercession for the needs of our family members and people we know, with petitionary prayer for our own, personal needs. This isn't a bad thing. But it narrows our horizons and constrains the power we have to effect changes in the world, that is unless we don't believe that Christian prayer is powerful and effective. In any case, the New Testament commands Christians to pray for those they don't know personally. As followers of Jesus, it is our responsibility to pray for those we don't know.

I raise the point because the letter to the Colossians opens with prayer for people the author doesn't know. The author reports that the Colossians have received the gospel from Epaphras who has reported their faith and love (v. 6). On the basis of what he's heard, the author prays for this church he hasn't visited. How he does that suggests three practical suggestions for prayers for "unknowns." First, the author prays with familial language (vv. 1–2). Second, he begins with thanksgiving (vv. 3–8), and, third, only then does he move on to petition (vv. 9–14).

The author opens with family language. Timothy is a "brother." The letter's recipients are "brethren" (or brothers and sisters), an interesting way to address people one hasn't met. Although the author hasn't yet visited Colossae, he thinks of the "saints" as his siblings.

Certainly Paul's letters indicate that baptized people have a special relationship to each other. We are baptized into Christ Jesus, made siblings to him and to each other. Christians are the sons and daughters of the same Father. This means *all* other Christians—whether we've met them or not—are our family, with all the responsibilities of love and duty that go along with biological family. This is a big order, and one we've not taken seriously enough in our history as church.

Pushing this point a bit, because of the Great Commission, the "go ye into all the world and preach the gospel" at the end of Matthew (28:19–20), everyone is a potential sibling-in-Christ. Even more radically, Jesus has commanded Christians to pray for our *enemies* and those who persecute (or even terrorize) us (Matt 5:44). Practically, this means that there's nobody for whom I am excused from praying. I have a special responsibility to pray for other Christians and an implicit responsibility to pray for everyone in the world.

Second, when the author takes up the task of praying for the Colossian Christians he doesn't know, he begins with Thanksgiving. Thanksgiving and petition go together in his mind. In Greek verses 3–8 are one long sentence giving the reasons why the author thanks God for the Colossians, because of their triad of great Christian virtues: faith, love and hope. Even the *rumor* of their virtues leads him to thank God, the source and end of all virtue. If someone has faith or love or hope, it is because God gave it (see Jas 1:17–18).

The gospel the Colossians heard, that has given them hope, is "bearing fruit and growing in the whole world." And it is bearing fruit among them, too. So the author thanks God that there is something to show for their reception of the gospel. The Book of James speaks of Christians showing what they believe by what they do (Jas 2:18–26). In Hebrew Scripture "to hear" and "to obey" are nearly synonymous. If one *hears* the gospel, the expectation is that she responds by *doing,* acting on the basis of, being obedient to what she has heard. This is exemplified after the Jews in Jerusalem heard Peter's Pentecost sermon and responded "what shall we *do?*" (Acts 2: 37, italics mine) "Bear fruit" is a biblical metaphor for "act." The "bearing fruit" image makes me wonder if the author doesn't have in mind the "fruits of the spirit" enumerated in Gal. 5:22: love, joy, peace, patience, kindness, generosity, faithfulness, gentleness, self-control. These are "outward and visible" proof of having heard the gospel and are "thank worthy."

Third, the author is thankful the Colossians have responded actively to what Epaphras preaches and so in vv. 9–14 intercedes for his unmet siblings. Basically, he prays that they will keep on, keeping on, continue to do what they *are* doing. Twice he prays for their growth in knowledge. He wants them to know God's will, to have spiritual wisdom and understanding and thus to live lives worthy of God "*bearing fruit in every good work.*" Paul prays that they will be strong with God's strength and "prepared to endure everything with patience."

This suggests that the fruit bearing in Colossae is going on in the midst of some difficulties, but the point here is that the author is thankful for and asking for (on behalf of) his Colossian siblings in the context of difficulty. Whatever this difficulty is, it must be serious because it leads the author to remind the Colossian Christians of the "saints in light," those in heaven or perhaps those *also* transferred into the Kingdom of his beloved son, to remind them that Christ has rescued them from the power of darkness and given them citizenship in Christ's kingdom.

Although the author knows that the Colossian church is enduring some trial, he doesn't ask God to take it away from them, just as Jesus in his "High Priestly Prayer" in John 17:15 doesn't ask God to take believers out of the world, but to protect them from the Evil One. What the author asks God to give the Colossian Christians is knowledge of God, spiritual wisdom and understanding, and Divine strength, all of which make it possible to "endure everything with patience, while joyfully giving thanks to the Father" (1:11–12). Why? Because in a mysterious way, they are *already* living in Christ's realm, no matter how messy, difficult, and dangerous this realm is.

How do we pray for people we don't know? First, we have to remember to pray for them at all. Colossians suggests we pray for them *as if* they were our siblings, our brothers and sisters, those very close to us, as, in fact, both because of modern media and spiritual reality, they are. Perhaps, for example, we would do well to pray with the morning paper or the weekly news magazine.

Second, we are to begin our prayers with thanksgiving for what we have heard that is *good* about the family we haven't met. We are invited to consider what might be good about our enemies or difficult "strangers." This is not Pollyanna. It's recognizing that all prayer begins with gratitude, if for no other reason than that we ask God for things because God has already done things for us. In gratitude for prayers answered in the past, we ask for future favors.

Finally, the author suggests that the spiritual virtues that lead us to pray thankfully for those we don't know, even for our enemies, are precisely what we should request for them. What better thing might I ask for a person other than that he or she know God's will and have strength to live it in patience, joy, and thanksgiving? In any situation to know and attempt to do God's will is the best we can hope for. The author thanks God for what's good about the Colossians; he prays they will have knowledge and strength to continue in to "walk in" God's way, then doubles back to close with thanksgiving for what the all-powerful God has already done in Christ. The prayer exhibits twice as much "thank you" as "give us" or "do," and this, itself, is an important, practical word.

In our world, it is crucial that we pray for all sorts of people we don't know. It's important for us to forge bonds of fellowship and friendship by thinking of unknown people as siblings instead of strangers or enemies. It's important to consider what's good about them, what we can thank God for, rather than what needs to be obliterated. It's crucial to pray that they, and we, have deeper knowledge of God's will and the strength to live and endure what God's will might mean in our day. And, in the midst of the difficulties and terrors and plain old cussedness of human history, it's most important to remember that we Christians already share the inheritance of the saints in light, that Christ has already triumphed, that we are already citizens of a much, much better Kingdom than any earthly one.

7

It's All about Jesus

(1:13–23)

TEXTUAL NOTES

Most of the textual matters in the Christ hymn of 1:15–20 have been treated in chapter 2 of Part One. Let us simply note here that the hymn is framed with soteriological passages, texts that describe God's saving work in Jesus. They are 1:12b–14 and 1:21–23. The first provides the bridge between the opening prayer and the hymn, and the second describes the relationship of the work of God in Christ to the Colossians, themselves. It opens "And, you" (1:21). It's a sort of "before" (v.21) and "after" (v. 22) with a proviso (v. 23). It compares what they were (estranged, hostile, and evil) with what they are now (holy, blameless, irreproachable) *provided that* they continue in the Pauline teaching declared to them by Epaphras (1:7–8). That Paul, if he is the author, is a servant of that gospel leads to a sort of biographical excursus on suffering in 1:24 to 2:5. But first, there is what I take to be the most important part of the letter: the Christ hymn.

REFLECTION ON THE PASSAGE

When all is said and done, it's really about Jesus. All the other things the church gets so roiled about are a distant second to Jesus: Who he is and our response to his Identity. "Who do you say that I am?" "What are you going to do about it?" are the important questions. Unfortunately, among the smorgasbord choices that constitute the modern church's doctrines and practices, and, indeed the multiplicity of religious life and the varieties of spirituality, it is all too easy for even Christians to forget the centrality of Jesus.

In first-century Colossae the author of the letter faced the equivalent of this in a church he hadn't visited. We seem to think that there were three religious choices at the time: Judaism, Christianity, and "Pagan," as if Christianity weren't a variety of Judaism and "Pagan" didn't include a multiplicity of Greco-Roman religions and spiritual choices. Paul began his missions by preaching in synagogues because he was a Jew. But the people to whom he preached had myriad ways to express what we now call their "spirituality."

This was part of the problem in Colossae and the reason for this letter to them. Believers apparently had begun to play fast and loose with the gospel Epaphras had preached. It's the problem some people call syncretism and others term "multiple religious belonging" that the author has in mind when he opens the body of the letter with a clear focus on Jesus. He demonstrates at the outset in the Christ hymn of 1:15–20 the superiority of Jesus over every other option. To put it crudely, it's the spiritual equivalent of "my dad can beat up your dad". "Our Jesus," says the author "has an origin and authority and extent that is greater than any other option going."

Colossians is a carefully organized epistle. After the salutation, thanksgiving and prayer, the author turns to speak of Jesus in 1:13–23a. Verses 13–14 are a hinge between the prayer and the Jesus material and introduce what God has accomplished by means of Jesus. Verses 15–20 are an inserted hymn that summarizes the importance of Jesus. Verses 13–14 speak in terms of God and of "us." Verses 15-20 shift to speak only of Christ. Verses 21-23 speak to "you," returning to what God has done in Jesus. So there's a "soteriological bracket," a frame around the Christ hymn which highlights it. What the author does here is a familiar technique of preachers. He quotes hymns or bits of liturgy with which those to whom he writes are familiar. Another clear example (on the same subject) is the Christ hymn in Phil 2:6-11. Paul, and preachers, use familiar material to reinforce their more important or difficult points.

Apparently from the beginning, Christians sang to and about Jesus. The church's earliest christology wasn't creeds, but hymns, acts of worship and praise. Singing engages the whole of a person. It helps us remember things. It helps us pray. (Parenthetically, this is why hymnody is so important: it gets into our bodies and forms us in its image.) If you want to know what a given congregation or parish *really* believes, don't look at its creeds or its mission statement, pay attention to the hymns the people love and sing frequently with gusto.

The author of Colossians chooses what must have been a well known hymn to remind the Colossians of what is essential about Jesus. One suggestions is that it has two stanzas: verses 15-18a deal with Christ and creation, and verses 18b-20 deal with Christ and reconciliation. The following is a list (discussed in much more detail on pp. 23-28 above) of seven important assertions the hymn makes about Jesus.

1. He is "the image of the invisible God." Jesus perfectly reveals God. In him all the fullness of God "was pleased to dwell."

2. He is the "firstborn of all creation." Jesus has primacy; he comes before everything else. And "firstborn" suggests there were other siblings in God's mind from the beginning.

3. In him, through him and for him all things were created. The hymn is speaking of Jesus's crucial agency in the whole, cosmic creation. Invisible, visible, dominions,

thrones, powers, they all, one way or another, came about through Jesus.

4. He is "before all things" bespeaks Jesus' temporal priority. Jesus is not only the first among siblings; he's the first among everything!

5. In him "all things hold together." Jesus not only brought everything into being, all being continues to exist because of him. Jesus is the principle of coherence in the universe. Without him, everything would fly apart. As the hymn writer understood it, without him there would be a "Big Bang" of destruction, not creation.

6. He is the head of the church. The hymn not only stresses the cosmic importance of Jesus; it reminds the Colossians of his primacy in the Church. Jesus is the church's authority figure and origin, because "head" is a biblical metaphor not only for "authority," but for "origin."

7. Finally, he is the first born from the dead. This is Good News! "First born" suggests that others follow. Just as Jesus was the agent of all of creation, he is the agent of re-creation, of resurrection.

The hymn reminds the Colossians of truths about Jesus. Then in vv. 21–23 the author of the letter tells them the implications for themselves. "You Colossians who used to be evil and estranged from God have now been reconciled to God through the death of the earthly Jesus." But there's a proviso: "*provided that you continue securely established and steadfast in the faith*" (1:23 italics mine). Some of you are drifting away from the gospel you heard from Epaphras. COME BACK!"

The author and Epaphras faced an error related to the way the Colossian Christians understood Jesus. So the author inserts a hymn in his letter that established Christ as first and supreme in creation. Thus all powers are subject to his lordship. The hymn reminds the Colossian Christians of who Jesus is and what he has accomplished. The author asserts that all the church needs, it has in Jesus.

No wonder "the heavens are telling the glory of God" (Ps 19:1): they are from and through and to Jesus. All the orderly processes of the universe are Christ connected. Christ has already effected a cosmic reconciliation of heaven and earth, matter and spirit, and of the light and darkness within each one of us. He has already liberated us from all that enslaves us: fear, doubt, disease, death, rulers, principalities, powers. Our task is to live the freedom that is already ours. Unfortunately, people prefer slavery and cultural servitude to the freedom of the sons and daughters of God.

I heard a story about a Native American woman who had to walk home alone after dark. Someone offered to accompany her so she wouldn't be afraid in the night. She replied, "no, I won't be afraid. We have songs for this." We, too have songs for the dark world and the historic night in which we now live. One of them is Col 1:15–20. It reminds us that not only has "Jesus paid it all," (in the words of a gospel hymn) but that he is before it all, its origin, agency, coherence, and authority, "so that he might come to have first place in everything" (v. 18).

This section of Colossians leaves us with consolation and a challenge. The consolation is the reminder of all that Christ is and has done. The challenge is to put him first in everything. The Christ of whom the early Church sang can, and wants, to take first place in us. But he can't take up residence until we make room for him. When we do so, we become living images of the Christ we carry, which is more or less what Paul wrote to the church at Corinth: "And all of us, with unveiled faces, seeing the glory of the Lord as though reflected in a mirror *are being transformed into the same image* from one degree of glory to another; for this comes for the Lord, the Spirit" (2 Cor 3:18, italics mine).

8

"Behold, I Tell You a Mystery"

(1:23b—2:7)

TEXTUAL NOTES

In his commentary, Pokorný calls this section "a digression because 2:6 connects both with 2:5 and 1:23. The part in between is
written in the first person singular."[168] Colossians 1:23—2:7 follows
from 1:21–23a, which focused on the changed status of the Colossian believers from estranged, hostile, and evil to holy, blameless,
and irreproachable. This is "provided that" (conditional upon)
their loyalty to the gospel they heard from Epaphras who heard
it from Paul (1:23). Before the author introduces the "confused
teachings" (2:8–23), he provides a biographical excursus which
colors what will follow (1:23b—2:7). Dunn explains it was "Paul's
custom to write about his own missionary labors and personal in-
volvement with his readers . . . after the opening thanksgiving . . .
but elsewhere also . . ."[169] For example, Paul followed this pattern
in Philippians, describing his personal circumstances in 1:15–30
before proceeding with the body of the letter.

Here the biographical section, especially 1:24—2:1, addresses
suffering in the Christian life. As did Christ, the author is suffering for the sake of others. (For more on 1:24, see the excursus on

pp. 35–37 above.) His sufferings are linked to those of Christ. This is part of the mystery of the gospel now revealed as the inclusion of the Gentiles (1:26–27). For this gospel the author toils and struggles and from it he receives internal empowerment. If this letter is not written by Paul, it is by one who knew the inner workings of his mind revealed in the "uncontested letters."

While 2:1–3 continue the first-person biography, they remind the reader of the earlier christology. Christ is God's mystery "in whom are hidden all the treasures of wisdom and knowledge" (2:2–3). Having been baptized into Christ, nothing else is required, even if a case for other requirements is made "with plausible arguments" (2:4), so 2:6–7 serve to introduce 2:8–15, a practical expansion of the christology presented in the hymn in 1:15–20. The "biographical excursus" stresses living life "in Christ" "as you were taught" by Epaphras (1:7), *not* by the "deceivers" (2:4) allusion to whose inaccurate teaching will follow in 2:8–23.

REFLECTION ON THE PASSAGE

The prophet Isaiah reminds us of what we all know: "my thoughts are not your thoughts, nor are your ways my ways, says the Lord" (55:8). To human understanding, God's ways are often unutterably mysterious. This idea informs this section of Colossians in which the author uses the potent word "mystery" three times. Some scholars call it a "digression" on Paul's ministry, as if he's wandered off from the Colossian church into his own concerns. Read carefully, one discovers many echoes of what the author prayed for the Colossians in 1:9–14 repeated here and in similar language.

The text is framed in 23b–25 and 2:1–5 with information about the author's situation. He describes himself as a suffering servant of the gospel "for your sake" (1:24). Twice he says he is a servant of the gospel. He is suffering and struggling for the Colossians and the Laodiceans and "all who have not seen me face to face" (2:1). Physically absent, he is with them in spirit and their "morale and the firmness of [their] faith in Christ" (2:5) encourage him. He accepted suffering on their behalf (note, the exact parallel of what Jesus did for them and for us) "so that no one may deceive you with plausible arguments" (2:4). False teaching is appearing in the Colossian church (more on that shortly). Here the author establishes a connection with the Colossians. They are suffering (1:11–12), and he is suffering, and suffering for them. They are, so to speak, in the "same boat."

In 1:25–28 and 2:2–3 the word "mystery" and some other very interesting language appears. Earlier we noted that Colossians had a multitude of religious and spiritual choices available. One of the most popular categories of religion in the Greco-Roman world, and in particular in Asia Minor (to which Colossae and Laodicea belong) was "Mystery Religions" or "The Mysteries." The basic idea in these traditions was that there is secret knowledge (*gnosis*) into which one can be initiated and thereby gain salvation. Behind the appeal is a very human characteristic: we are curious about what is hidden. As children we hunted for our Christmas presents before Christmas. It's why some folks are interested in Masonic organizations, sororities, fraternities. There are hidden things we don't know but might learn as initiates.

What the author very cleverly does here is to use the vocabulary of Mystery Religions with reference to Jesus Christ. It's an example of his "dual purpose vocabulary." In the face of multiple religious choices in Colossae and Ephesus, the author uses terms the Greco-Romans will recognize, but fills them with new meaning in a Christian context. Mystery, hidden, revealed, wisdom, understanding, knowledge: all of these are technical terms in Mystery Religions. They are also what the author (and presumably Epaphras) has been telling, and continues to tell, the Colossians are theirs in Christ Jesus.

Having established his connection with them as one who is also suffering for the gospel, the author suggests that Christianity, too, has its mysteries. (Indeed, some people thought Christianity was another Mystery Religion.) But the hidden is now revealed and available to everyone. "[T]he mystery that has been hidden throughout the ages and generations . . . has now been revealed to his saints" (1:26). "I want their hearts to be encouraged . . . so that they may have . . . assured understanding . . . of God's mystery" (2:2).

What is the content of the now-revealed mystery? It is twofold. First, 2:2–3 says "God's mystery, that is, Christ himself, in whom are hidden all the treasures of wisdom and knowledge." God's mystery is the all-sufficient Christ about whom they sing in their hymn in 1:15–20. Second, according to 1:27, God makes known to *gentiles* (a most remarkable assertion for a Jewish scholar if the author is Paul[170]) "The riches of the glory of this mystery, which is Christ in you, the hope of glory." As Jean-Pierre de Caussade noted so long ago "Faith sees that Jesus Christ lives in everything and works through all history to the end of time, that every fraction of a second, every atom of matter, contains a fragment of his hidden life and his secret activity. The actions of created beings are veils which hide the profound mysteries of the workings of God."[171]

The mystery is Christ *within* the Colossians, and within us. "Christ in you, the hope of glory" is an arresting phrase, an amazing idea. The author asserts that that, upon our confession of Jesus Christ and our baptism into his death and resurrection, he lives *in* us. We are living, breathing containers of Christ (see also 1 Cor 6:19). Christ is the *ikon* of God, and we are the *ikon* of Christ.

The great missionary to North Africa, Charles de Foucauld had a profound understanding of and devotion to this point. He wrote Jesus "is near me, this perfect Being, who is All Being, who is the one true Being, who is all Beauty, goodness, wisdom, love, knowledge, intelligence." He continues "you are in me and around me, You fill me altogether . . . there is no particle of my body that you do not fill, and around me you are nearer than the air in which I move."[172] Living among Muslims in North Africa, Foucauld probably knew the beautiful teaching from the Holy Qu'ran that God is nearer to us than our juggler vein. The Christian assertion is even more radical. It is that the Lord of the universe chooses to make his throne room in the hearts of his servants. In Jesus, God's hidden and mysterious ways are made known in us in whom by grace he chooses to dwell.

God's mysteries are revealed in Jesus. We more or less "get that." But what are the practical implications of the mystery of Christ resident within us? One is that the body is important. "Evil flesh, good spirit" is not Christian thinking. (It's not Pauline thinking, either.) It's Gnostic, another of those religious choices in first-century Asia Minor. Christianity teaches that our bodies are important, so important that God assumed one. In the incarnation, God divinized human flesh, which means that what we do in and with the body matters. Our health and weight and sexuality matter because they are part of the preparation for Christ the "inner guest." Paul wrote in 1 Corinthians very directly about these matters.

Much of the great devotional literature and spiritual theology of the Christian tradition speak of our interior life as a room in which Jesus dwells. St. Teresa of Avila devoted a book to this, appropriately named *The Interior Castle.* Not only is the care of the physical body a matter of theological importance, but the "furnishings" of our interior life are the "furnishings" we are providing for Jesus the Interior Guest. What kind of interior space are we providing for Jesus Christ? With what are we filling our minds and hearts? What do you think about? What sort of music do you listen to? What kinds of TV programs and movies do you watch? What kind of language do you use? What do you read?

A lot of us treat our interior lives like an attic or cellar. We just keep shoving old stuff in there. Unless we clean it out, it won't go away. In order for Jesus to take up residence, we must make room for him. For some of us that's going to mean throwing away some old, moldy junk that doesn't belong there any more: old resentments and angers, judgmentalism, prejudices. It's hard work carting that stuff out of our psychic basement. But once it's out we can re-decorate with fruits of the spirit that make Christ comfortable: love, joy, peace, patience, kindness, humility, self-control (Gal 5:22–23). Furnishing with these spiritual virtues is our way of putting out the welcome mat for Jesus who wants to come in and help us finish the interior redecoration.

The author of Colossians is telling those Christians that God's hidden ways have now been revealed to them in Jesus Christ who wants to take up residence within them. That is their "hope of glory." They had, and we have, a little interior cleaning to do before Jesus arrives.

9

"You Were Buried with Him in Baptism"

(2:4–15)

TEXTUAL NOTES

The Colossian letter is particularly well organized and synthetic. It is difficult to divide the text into discrete units. For example, the biographical material in 1:23—2:5 moves seamlessly and logically into the author's concern about teaching not from Epaphras (2:4–23). On the basis of his biography, the author establishes his authority to speak to a community he's not met. Then 2:4–6 introduce one of the most closely examined sections of the letter, 2:8–23. Many scholars extract from it material to support theories of the identity of the "false teachers" in Colossae, teachers whose message is opposed to that of Epaphras.

In 2:8–15 the author presents the practical implications of the Christ hymn (1:15–20) to the Colossians' situation. Those verses are framed by references to captivity ("takes you captive" in v. 8, and the image of a triumphal procession in v. 15) suggesting the "alternative teachings" set forth by the other teachers represent imprisonment. The comparison is between what is human and temporal and what is divine and permanent and is grounded in assertions about Christ (1:15–20) and their own new reality as those baptized "in him," characterized as "spiritual circumcision" (2:11). (Readers of Paul's letters will recall the great concern with circumcision in Galatians, and also, I hope, note the very different tone of the author of Colossians.)

Colossians 2:6–15 are a series of images familiar in the Greco-Roman world: vv. 6–7 remind them of the teaching received from Epaphras; vv. 8 and 15 frame the discussion by reference to cosmic powers ("elemental spirits of the universe" and "rulers and authorities"); vv. 9–10 contain many verbal allusions to the Christ hymn; vv. 11–12 are baptism images; and vv. 13–14 use the language of economics, specifically cancellation of debt.

REFLECTION ON THE PASSAGE

In many Christian traditions people are baptized not as infants, but at an age when it can become their choice to submit to baptism. They often remember vividly their baptisms, as the Colossian Christians would have done. If you can't remember your baptism, can you describe what it means? What does it mean to be *baptized into* Christ Jesus? This appeal to the memory and meaning of baptism is at the heart of the letter to the Colossian church, a letter which Käsemann argued was part of an early Christian baptismal liturgy.[173]

The primary reason the writer addresses the Colossians whom he does not know is that he has heard of their faith and of challenges to it. Teachers are trying to deceive them with "plausible arguments." Whatever the false teaching, and a great deal of ink has been spilled trying to define it, it isn't goofy, wacky, silly, or outrageous. It's "plausible," reasonable, believable. That's why it's so dangerous. The author refers to it as "philosophy." Not one to pull punches, he also calls it "empty deceit" (2:8).

Colossians reflects a mysterious controversy that has to do with Jesus. Opponents to what Epaphras taught (i.e., Paul's Gospel), whomever they were—Pythagorean philosophers or Gnostics or syncretistic Jews have been proposed—taught a "philosophy"

(2:8) in accordance with the "elements of the universe" (2:8) and the "worship of angels" (2:18), Jewish cultic practices (2:16) and ascetic rigor (2:21–23). We'll deal with those details in the next reflection. This one focuses on the response to syncretistic false teachers who combine elements of Judaism with elements found in Greco-Roman paganism.

Not surprisingly, the response is to reprise yet again in vv. 9–10 the chief point of the Christ hymn quoted at the outset. The response to the plausible philosophers is to stress the absolute supremacy of Christ who is superior to any other supernatural beings, who, in fact, have no authority but are captives in Christ's triumphal procession. The image in v. 15 is of the Roman practice of marching the spoils of war and the captives of war through city streets. It was a way of humiliating the losers and assuring Roman citizens of the glories of Rome.

In the frame between the pictures of Christ's supremacy in vv. 9–10 and 15, the central image is of baptism, not how it is *done* (its form), but what it *means*. "You were circumcised with a spiritual circumcision" (2:11). "Circumcision" has to be a metaphor because Paul had argued so vehemently against it in Galatians, and because Colossians is likely to be a predominantly gentile church. (And, of course, female Christians, some of whom Paul praised as leaders in the churches, couldn't receive Jewish circumcision, which was exclusionary.) Verse 12 makes this clear: "you were buried with him in baptism" and "raised with him through faith in the power of God, who raised him from the dead." Paul used this same dramatic image in Romans 6: "we have been buried with [Christ] by baptism into death, so that, just as Christ was raised from the dead by the glory of the Father, so we too might walk in newness of life" (Rom 6:4).

Whatever else baptism is, it is a matter of death and life. Paul always describes baptism as a process of death to life. Here, to a Gentile church, the author can write that they were dead in trespasses against the law because they weren't circumcised bodily as Jews (2:13). In spite of that, in baptism, God forgave them and made them alive, "chose them" as it were. Verse 14, which describes this, employs an unusual word, *cheirographon*: a certificate of indebtedness issued by a debtor in his own writing to acknowledge debt. (See excursus on pp. 35–37 above.) This is what Christ nailed to the cross. Human beings owed God a huge debt. Metaphorically, we had maxed out all our spiritual credit cards. What Christ did was cancel our debt and resurrect our credit rating with God. Baptism is how we "get out of debt free."

This is not only a theological matter, but one with crucial practical implications. First, baptism means that we no longer belong primarily to ourselves (or to our parents or to our spouses or to our nations), but to Jesus Christ. As Paul said in 1 Corinthians "you are not your own." "For you were bought with a price" (6:19–20 and 7:23). You know what kind of human being is bought with a price? Slaves. Again, Paul wrote in 1 Corinthians "whoever was free when called is a slave of Christ . . ." (7:22). The language in the New Testament of being slaves, as shocking as it sounds to us, is precisely correct, because it is understood that we were *bought* by the death and resurrection of Jesus. He owns us, has the right to tell us what to do, and expect our obedience. The happy side-effect of being so purchased is salvation, which is not something we get when we die, but something we have right now: "you *have come* to fullness in him" (2:10, italics mine). Christ is already *in* us "the hope of glory" (1:27, italics mine). We are "saved" now.

Second, and related, baptism means that we really *are* forgiven: "he forgave us all our trespasses, erasing the record that stood against us" (2:13–14). It's odd, but one of the hardest things for human beings to accept is that we are loveable, and we are forgiven *already,* and not for anything we have done or could do. Perhaps the hardest concept in Christianity is not incarnation or justification or any of the other "ations" no matter how difficult. It's grace, unmerited favor shown to us by God.

God forgives us not because of who we are and have or have not done, but because of who God is. It's God's nature to create, to give life, to love what is created and living, to love it and to forgive it when it falls short of that love. Sin, at its root, is ignorance of how much God loves, of God's nature as love. Mostly sinners are people who don't know they're loved. You don't have to "act hateful" (as it was described in my youth) when you are secure that you are loved and forgiven. Baptism is a cosmic bath. Everything the individual and the human family has done against God's love is washed away in water, the symbol of life and of God's ongoing giving of it in love. Whatever we did (and most of us did some doozies!), baptism means it's over with, done, finished. Baptism means we really are forgiven and eternally loved.

Third, and finally (and as we've noted before), baptism profoundly relates us to every other baptized person. Paul often uses sibling language to describe Christians' relationships to each other. A practical and not altogether easy side effect of belonging to Christ in baptism is that I also belong to every other baptized person, and they belong to each other and to me. Baptism ends "me and Jesus." Once a person is baptized it has to be "we and Jesus" and "us together." This is clear in the second person pronoun the author uses in this passage; it's plural ("you" plural). When Jesus teaches us to pray it's always in the plural: *our* Father, *our* daily bread, *our* trespasses, lead *us* not into temptation, deliver *us* from evil. You get the point. This idea of *communio* is one of the helpful and creative premises in Margaret MacDonald's commentary on Colossians.[174]

If, practically speaking, the hardest Christian *concept* is grace (accepting God's love and forgiveness), the hardest Christian practice is *koinonia*, common life. We not only belong to Jesus. We belong to each other with all of the joy and difficulty, responsibility and exasperation that entails. Except in very healthy monastic communities and some communal groups of the radical Reformation, Christian history demonstrates we have never understood this well or acted on it effectively. This is why the author of Colossians is worried about plausible false teachers in Colossae. What we believe matters because we act on the basis of what we believe. How different human history would be if Christians had understood, believed, and acted on the cosmic implications of baptism.

10

Principles of Discernment

(2:16—3:4)

TEXTUAL NOTES

"Therefore" in v. 16 indicates that what follows arose from what preceded it. Having established the power of God and Jesus Christ in 2:8–15, the author now gives a series of concrete examples of the "philosophy and empty deceit" introduced in 2:8. The warning in 2:16–17 employs the Platonic language of shadow and substance. The language of 2:18–19 is particularly strong and repeats the language of the Christ hymn (1:17b–18a) and the immediately preceding section (2:9) in referring to "the head." Christ the head is the unifying factor in his body, the believing community. The Greek construction of verse 20 presumes the affirmative answer, follows from 2:12–19, and anticipates 3:1.

The three principles of discernment for evaluating teaching appear in 2:22–23: The first is to determine whether a teaching is of human or of divine origin, of humans or from Christ. Second, are the teachings temporal or eternal? Do they have only human or eternal consequences? Third, do the teachings actually *empower* one to keep them? The author of Colossians does not want the Colossian Christians to waste their lives on what perishes and does not empower. (Compare 1 Cor 9:25; 15:42; 2 Cor 4:18 and John 6:27.) The writer again defends the all sufficiency of Christ whose complete authority was established in 1:15–20. The Colossian Christians have entered into that authority through baptism (2:11–14) and become part of the body of which Christ is the head.

The implicit comparison in 3:1—4:6 is between what the recipients of the letter *were* and what they are now through baptism into Christ. The transition from teachings that require temporal and un-necessary actions to instructions on the practical implications of baptism occur in 3:1–4. Since they have been "raised with Christ in baptism," (3:1) the Colossian Christians are to set their minds on or be "minded toward" (*phroneite*, a term that was importantly used by Paul in teachings to the Philippian church) "above things." They have died (in baptism) and are now, for a season (3:4), "hidden with Christ in God," (3:3), the simple pronouncement of a mystical reality. All the practical instructions and imperatives in 3:5—4:6 follow from this.

REFLECTION ON THE PASSAGE

How should we make decisions when there are "plausible arguments" for something, "plausible arguments" like those the Colossian Christians were hearing from teachers other than Epaphras and those who taught the Pauline gospel? How to make difficult decisions about beliefs and the actions that result from them is at the heart of the letter to the Colossians. Some groups of rival teachers were teaching a "philosophy" different from the gospel taught by Epaphras and Paul. In this section of the letter, we learn something of what it entailed and of the author's response to it.

These teachers were making "plausible arguments" in favor of dietary laws ("food and drink" v. 16), and certain religious holidays ("festivals, new moons, Sabbaths" v. 16). They were interested in ascetic practices ('self-abasement" v. 18, "do not handle, taste, touch" v. 21, and "severe treatment of the body" v. 23), and unusual kinds of worship experiences ("worship of angels" and "visions" v. 18). Colossians' author argues that these may have "an appearance of wisdom" but they are really of "no value" (v. 23). How does he know? How can he be so sure? What are his principles of discernment?

Although it is a little oblique, at the heart of the Colossian letter is the matter of discernment, how Christians make decisions, how we recognize or perceive things. "Discern," like so many English words, is Latinate. It is formed from *dis* meaning "apart" (as in *dis*tance or *dis*sociate) and *cernere* meaning "to separate." To be discerning is to be able to separate out the parts, to recognize differences. That is what the author of Colossians is up to here. He wants the Colossians to recognize the differences between the rival teachers and Epaphras and himself. What does he object to or find false about the "plausible arguments" of the rival teachers? And, second, what are his principles of discernment? What made him decide the rival teaching was "empty deceit" (v. 8)?

There are four basic things the author finds fault with in the rival teachers. First, he suggests these rival teachings aren't permanent. They are "only a shadow of what is to come" (v. 17; note the Platonic character of the language), and they "perish with use" (v. 22). Second, and relatedly, they "belong to the world" (v. 20) and so, by nature, they are passing away, impermanent. "The world" is not bad; it *is* temporal, impermanent. As the first and second objections are related, so are the third and fourth. The rival teachings are "human:" "A human way of thinking" (v. 18) and "simply human commands and teachings" (v. 22). These teachings may be clever and plausible, but their origin is human as opposed to heavenly or divine. They don't (the fourth objection) hold "fast to the head, from whom the whole body . . . grows with a growth that is from God" (v. 19). The author objects to the origin of the false teaching which isn't of divine origin. It isn't "from God."

What were his principles of discernment? How did he make his decisions about the falsity of these four ideas? Put positively, what characterizes teaching with which the writer would agree? Again, the passage suggests four principles. First, such teaching would in "substance" belong "to Christ" (v. 17). That is a way of saying that, for a Christian, a true or correct teaching would have its origins in the words and life of Jesus. It's "substance" or essence would be in accordance with what we know of what Jesus said and did. As such, the teaching's origin would be divine/heavenly. More on that in a moment.

Second, and related, such a teaching holds "fast to the head" (v. 19). That is, a Christian teaching would cling to the "head" of the Body (the church) whom the letter has made clear is Christ. The really important question for a Christian to ask in evaluating a teaching or practice is "Does this teaching or practice compromise the Lordship/Headship of Jesus in my life?" If there is any question that it might, it's probably best to reject it. Third, the author gives a very practical principle of discernment: "Does this give growth?" That which holds fast to the "head" "grows with a growth that is from God" (v. 19). As Creator, God is a God of life, and the basic characteristic of life is growth. Ideas and teachings and practices that are from God are always life giving and growth encouraging.

Finally, the author suggests that appropriate Christian teachings and practices are "from above." He repeats the word "above" twice in two verses at the beginning of chapter 3. "Above" suggests both divine origin and, because of divine origin, permanence, two things that the rival teachers' message do *not* exhibit. For the author, truth is divine and permanent, not human and passing. Clearly, the author compares "worldly things" or "human things" with "above things" or "heavenly things." The reader is not to conclude that what is earthly is bad and what is heavenly is good. That would insult God who (as Genesis and many Psalms assert) created what is earthly. The point is not that the world and the human are "bad," but that they are impermanent, ephemeral, passing away. The author does not want Colossian Christians to invest themselves, their energies, and their lives in ideas and practices that are temporary, but in those that are eternal. He doesn't want them to "labor for the food that perishes" (as Jesus put it in John 6:27).

This is an important principle for Christians and the church as an institution in every age to grasp. We must invest our energies in what lasts, not what is passing fad and fashion. Why, for example, argue (as many good Church folks did in the late twen-tieth century) about praise choruses as opposed to traditional hymns? These are matters of taste and fashion. Better that we invest ourselves in aspects of belief and practice that will never change: the truth of the saving death and resurrection of Jesus, the truth of the life and New Life God wants to give, the unchang-ing importance of baptism and of the Lord's Supper/Eucharist, of prayer and of Scripture.

The author strives to impress on the Colossians that, as a re-sult of their baptism (that image and practice that is so important in this letter and in Paul's letter to the Romans), they, in fact, are living in a new spiritual *environment* or *milieu*. Although still *in* the world, they are no longer *of* the world, "worldly" people. They live in Christ, are "rooted and built up in him" (2:6–7) . The open-ing of chapter 3 summarizes the first two chapters and presents the principles underlying the practical teachings that immediately follow. The point is that in baptism people "have been raised with Christ" (3:1); "you have died, and your life is hidden with Christ in God" (3:3).

Baptized people are no longer worldly people. The things that characterize "the world": perishability (what we might call "fash-ion" and "fad"), impermanence, things of purely human origin, the baptized need to treat very lightly, indeed. The really important question the author raises quite simply in v. 20 is "why do you live as if you still belonged to the world?" Why *do* we live as if we belonged to (that is are *owned by* because that's what "belong to" means) the world and had to follow all the passing fancies of its fads and fashions in things and in thought?

We belong to Christ who bought us. As Paul reminded the Corinthian Christians "you are not your own"; "For you were bought with a price . . ." (1 Cor 6:19–20). As the reader of the letter knows from 2:14, Christ paid off their debts (see the excursus on *cheirographon* on pp. 35–37 above), and thereby bought them. In their decision making, their task and principle should be to "hold fast to the head" which is the source of life and growth, to set the mind, not on ephemeral and worldly things, but on "things that are above" where Christ is "seated at the right hand of God" and where all that is permanent and permanently joy and life giving is to be found. "Why do you live as if you still belonged to the world?" (2:20); "you have received Christ Jesus the Lord, continue to live your lives in him, rooted and built up in him and established in the faith, . . . abounding in thanksgiving" (2:6–7).

11

What Easter Asks

(3:1–4)

TEXTUAL NOTES

For the context of 3:1–4, please see textual notes on 2:16—3:4 (the preceding section) or 3:5–18 (the following section). The reflection that follows links these teachings to Easter and the Pascal mystery.

REFLECTION ON THE TEXT

Although it seems obvious, it's worth remembering that, not only for Christians, but for the whole human family, Easter is a time of great rejoicing. I say "the whole human family" because Jesus said there were sheep not of his flock, and they, of course, are the Christian's responsibility to gather in (John 6:16). But for those who *have* heard the Shepherd's voice call us by name (John 6:3–4), Easter changes everything and cosmically for the better.

Easter is God's promise that death does not win and is not the end, but a new beginning. The resurrection of Jesus is not only promissory of eternal life for humans who "hear his voice" and respond, but, as the Apostle Paul so clearly understood, of the renewal of the whole creation which is "groaning in travail" waiting for it (Rom 8:22). Those in the northern hemisphere see that incipient restitution every spring in the bursting forth of daffodils and primroses in our gardens and the gamboling of lambs in the fields, lambs whose exuberance we might be wise to imitate in our Easter worship. The biblical theme in Holy Week is that of journeying as the Passover and Exodus from Egypt of the Hebrews is linked to our own paschal pilgrimage from death and darkness to life and light. Easter salvation is a home-going after wandering. We are sheep being drawn into the safety of God's fold.

Another biblical theme, that of gardens, also suggests God's benevolent plan. God put the human family into the Garden of Eden, and the human family didn't respond very well to God's generosity. Nevertheless, John in his Revelation is given a vision of heaven as a verdant garden. And the link between these two scriptural "book end" gardens are the gardens of Gethsemane (where Jesus' decision over-rides Adam and Eve's) and of the Empty Tomb, the Easter Garden where it all begins anew with a clean slate, an unblotted copy book.

All of this is what Easter *gives* us: new life, renewed creation, the reminder that we are now partially in an eternal life that will one day be ours in fullness. Resurrection is proof of God's power to make all things new (Rev 21:5; 2 Cor 5:17). Its reality gives us and is the source of our hope. No wonder the angel's first word to the myrrh bearing women was "Do not be afraid." But what does Easter *ask* of us? In one of his teaching sessions the Lukan Jesus says to his disciples "From everyone to whom much has been given, much will be required . . . (Luke 12:48). What more could we have been given than all that Easter promises? What does this divine generosity require or ask of us?

What Easter asks of us is spelled out quite clearly in Colossians: "if you have been raised with Christ [as noted earlier, the Greek construction is one that implies a positive response along the lines of *and you have*], seek the things that are above, where Christ is . . . Set your minds on things that are above, not on things that are on earth" (3:1–2). Easter asks of us a reorientation of consciousness, a redirection of our aspirations.

Having been raised with Christ in baptism (alluded to in Colossians by the Pauline metaphor from Romans 6 "you have died,"
that is, been buried and raised from the waters of baptism), our
inner lives are to be "Christ-directed." We are to "set our minds
on things that are above." "Above" is a Semitic metaphor for "the
heavenly world." The word for "setting of the mind" (*phroneite/ ph-
roneo*) is revelatory. To be "minded" a certain way is to have what
we might call a certain disposition, or temperament, or outlook.
Colossians suggests that our internal orientation be "above" not
"earthly." Easter asks us to examine our minds, our internal lives
and their aspirations.

What do we normally think about and aspire to? Are we
"minded" toward earthly things like power over others or wealth
or professional achievement or personal ego gratification? Paul's
list of "earthly mindedness" later in Colossians 3 isn't very pretty.
It includes fornication, impurity, passion, evil desire, and greed
(which he calls "idolatry" because, in fact we make "little gods"
of what we are greedy for), anger, wrath, malice, slander, abusive
language and lying. Or are we "minded toward" the "above things"
that characterized the life of our crucified and risen Lord: service,
humility, all-inclusive love that hopes and works for the welfare of
others regardless of the cost to ourselves? Paul speaks of "above
things" in a list that includes compassion, kindness, humility,
meekness, patience, bearing with others, forgiving, loving, allowing the peace of Christ to rule in our hearts. In Romans Paul said
that "those who live according to the Spirit set their minds on the
Spirit" and that mindedness "is life and peace" (8:5–6).

Paradoxically, Easter asks us to die to a lot of things the world
would ask us to live for. Easter asks us to be the leaven the in the
world's sodden loaf. Some of us still enjoy Easter baking, and we
know how transformative a teaspoon or two of yeast can be. Easter
asks us to be that yeast, to be the transformative person in our
families, our work places, our clubs and organizations, even in
our churches. Only one "above minded person," one person who
has taken to heart the great promises of Easter and no longer lives
from the demands of ego and the darkness of fear, can make an

enormous difference in her ordinary circumstances, in the lives of those he or she touches.

A great English poet, the nineteenth century Jesuit priest Gerard Manley Hopkins, wrote a poem about a ship wreck that focuses on how the behavior of five nuns changed the character of that tragedy. In the final stanza he prays: "Let him [that is, Christ] easter in us, be a dayspring to the dimness of us, / be a crimson-cresseted east . . ."[175] Hopkins recognized that the resurrection of Jesus asks that the noun "Easter" become in us the verb "to easter." Easter asks us to give our lives to "eastering." In each of us, our deepest most essential self is the life "hidden with Christ in God." Like the yeast mysteriously working in the dough to transform it, that hidden life in us can easter into a transformative energy, a powerful force for good and godliness in a world that is desperately in need of "above things."

Our Easter acclamation declares that Christ *has* been raised. We believe this. It is the locus of our hope. Colossians asserts that Christ *is* seated at God's right hand, the place of honor, in glory, and, wonder of wonders, it says that *we* have been raised with Christ. Already raised. Now. Maria Boulding puts it this way "the love we encounter face to face at the end is enfolding us now . . . continually asking us to open our hearts and receive."[176] Easter has given us so very, very much. And it asks us to do exactly what has been done for us, what our Lord has done: to give away what we have been given. Christ is risen; let him easter in us.

12

The Heart's Umpire

(3:5-17)

Colossians 3:1-17 presents what is important and necessary as counter to the unimportant and unnecessary requirements of the misguided teachings in 2:8-23. "Things that are above" (3:1) are more important than the earthly impermanent teachings previously critiqued by the author. There follows elaboration on "earthly things" to be "put to death" (3: 5-9, 11) and "heavenly things" to be "put on" (3:12-17). It is a program for Christian formation from the inside out. Christians are not to be reactive people, but those who live from inner convictions. The controlling image is, again baptismal, that of taking off and putting on (3:9, 10, 12, 14), and the implicit comparison is between who they were before Christ/ baptism and who they are after.

The passage is structured by vice and virtue lists (see pp. 43-45). Verse 5 is a vice list dominated by sexual sins. Verses 8-9a are a vice list dominated by sins of the tongue. They are "balanced" by a virtue list in verse 12 which functions as the *peripeteia*, the reversal in this passage. Because they have been raised with Christ (3:1) and *are* "God's chosen ones, holy and beloved" (3:12), they must exhibit behavior consonant with their new state of being. There follows a series of imperatives for positive behavior in vv. 13–16. (Remember that in uncontested Pauline letters, Paul never forbids an action without providing a positive alternative.) The vices condemned are actions that damage life in community, the virtues recommended those that facilitate it. The exhortations to virtuous action (especially the ones on prayer and worship in 3:16–17) are seamlessly continued in 4:2–6, suggesting that the material in 3:18—4:1 is an insertion.

REFLECTION ON THE PASSAGE

I'm not a football fan, but I come from a family who very definitely were. Saturday afternoons were sacred to college football. Even my mother, who in every other way was every inch the lady, would from time to time forget herself and be heard to yell from her demure seat on the couch "get 'em, get 'em, get 'em" in a very un-lady like tone of voice. To survive in my family, you needed to understand the umpire's signals. No one would break concentration from the game to explain what they meant. For the game to be understood and played properly, one had to understand and obey the referee.

The literal translation of the first phrase of Col 3:15 is "and the peace of Christ referee [or "umpire"] in your hearts." The Apostle Paul was apparently a sportsman. Many of his letters use imagery from the gymnasium and arena. He speaks of straining forward like a runner toward the finish line and of winning the laurel crown of the victor in the games. Here the author of Colossians also uses a verb found in ancient sports literature that means "umpire." The author tells the Colossians the peace of Christ must "call the shots" or "be the official" in their hearts. What if Jesus Christ were the heart's umpire, if he called the shots and made the decisions instead of our own preferences and prejudice and self-interest? How would churches be different if Christians submitted to Christ the umpire? How might that change our country and our world?

In Colossians 3 the author gives instructions for life after baptism. He begins "you have been raised with Christ" (3:1), an image of arising from the waters of baptism by immersion. He's speaking at least to some Greco-Romans who apparently didn't live (or perhaps know about?) the high moral rectitude of Judaism's Torah, to people whose morality was formed in a pagan environment. The author imagines them in a process of changing clothes as people literally did at baptism when they put off their old robes and donned the white robes of the baptized. They are going to have to take off a lot: fornication, impurity, evil desire, greed, anger, wrath, malice, slander, bad language. The author calls this "stripping off the old self" (3:9). But even in a pagan city you can't just strip off and stand around naked. You've got to put some clothes back on. So the author describes the "new clothes": "beloved, clothe yourselves with compassion, kindness, humility, meekness, patience . . ." (3:12). "Above all, clothe yourselves with love . . ." (3:14). Love alone brings harmony, another word for peace. (And note, that these attributes are all characteristics of Jesus, himself.)

"And let the peace of Christ umpire in your hearts, to which also you were called in one body and be thankful" (3:15). This verse summarizes the chapter to this point. "The peace of Christ" is the subject of the sentence, the "doer." What do we know about Christ's peace? We know from the Lord, himself, that it isn't the absence of conflict, the "put our feet up and rest" sort of peace. At the end of his life, in John's version of the "upper room" story, Jesus promises his friends who are facing a life shattering crisis "Peace I leave with you; my peace I give to you. I do not give to you as the world gives" (John 14:27). At the end of this Farewell Sermon to them he says "I have said this to you, so that in me you may have peace" (16:33).

The peace of Christ is a divine promise, but is "not of this world". It isn't what politicians or psychologists call peace, not absence of conflict between nations or within one's own life. It isn't of our own making. It comes as a gift, not an accomplishment. The NRSV adds the verb "let" (that is "allow") to v. 15 which is helpful because it indicates that the peace of Christ is something one must allow or invite in. If we ask, it will be given.

The peace which is promised when one allows Christ to "umpire" is superior to anything the human intellect can understand. In fact, it's not "rational" at all. Its locus is the "heart." In biblical anthropology, the heart is not the seat of emotional life. It is the metaphor for the core of personhood, the center the "true self," of willing and thinking and feeling. "Heart" is the whole person in his or her deepest aspect. This deepest aspect of self *must* submit to the "calls" of Christ the umpire. Christ must be the referee in every individual heart that calls itself Christian.

But the call to allow Christ to be umpire is, according to Col 3:15, a *communal* call. The author says that submission to Christ is that "to which you [plural] were called in one body." The church is in mind. The invitation is to the believing community. Christ's rule of peace is a rule over a people, indeed, the vocation of a people: "to which you [plural] *were called.*" "Were called" is a passive verb which suggests two things. First, something is being done *to* the ones called. They are not the "actor;" God is. In the New Testament when a Jewish writer uses the passive voice it's often a "Divine passive." Jews didn't say the Divine Name. A passive verb is a circumlocution, a roundabout way to say that God is the actor.

Here, the point is that God has called the Body of Christ to the vocation of being the community whose hearts have the peace of Christ as umpire. The church is called to be open to a rule and a way that is "out of this world," that is, in fact, completely misunderstood by this world. If Christians accept our calling, I guarantee you, we will change the world. But it will cost us individually. In speaking of "the aim of Jesus' preaching of the reign of God," Br. David Steindl-Rast, OSB notes "When we follow Jesus it means that we take up our own crosses, because following Jesus quite explicitly means undermining the ruling order of society, even today. That is something radically Revolutionary."[177] What if the umpire of every Christian heart were the love of Jesus Christ who loved to the end and went to the cross of Calvary in love and for love?

The peace the author alludes to here is precisely what allowed an innocent man to stand up to the false accusation of a corrupt political and religious system. That peace allowed him to stand silently when accused and beaten. That peace allowed him to pick up the cross and stumble to Calvary and stretch out his hands and feet to receive the nails. That peace allowed him to say to the thief beside him "This day you will be with me in paradise" (Luke 23:43), and of those who killed him, "Father, forgive them; they don't know what they are doing" (Luke 23:34). And on the third day in the garden of resurrection, that peace exploded as a power in the universe—and became available to us. The "peace of Christ" is out of this world, but it's *for* this world, and the world will only receive it if we allow him who incarnated it to umpire in us.

The peace of Christ is unaffected by the external events of life; it "passes understanding." Indeed, those who exhibit such peace are living conundrums in our world. How can they be so quietly serene and so deeply committed in the face of the turmoil and suffering that is life in this world? Not because of anything they do, but because of the one *in whom* they live, the one who "calls their shots," Who is the umpire of their hearts.

"And the peace of Christ rule in your hearts to which you were called in one body. *And be thankful*" (3:15, italics mine). For the author of Colossians, the peace of Christ and gratitude go hand in hand. One can't force it, or earn it, or make it because it is free to whomever will accept it. And that gift is great cause for gratitude. Christians are the people, the body, to whom God has promised the peace of his Christ. Peace is the gift, and the appropriate response is gratitude.

13

"As Is Fitting in the Lord"

(3:18—4:6)

TEXTUAL NOTES

This unit of material closes the second teaching unit of Colossians. It is composed of a household code (see chapter three above) and a final parenesis in the form of *topoi*, short, pithy instructions. The household code of 3:18—4:1 is shorter than that in Eph 5:21—6:9 (which probably followed it), but more complete than the one in 1 Pet 3:1–7. That the longest instruction is to slaves (4 of 9 verses) suggests both that there were many slaves in the Colossian church and that the relationship between them and their masters was difficult, probably made more so if both were Christians. Perhaps the most universal teaching in the code is the instruction to do all work as if it were for the Lord. The passage is *not* justification for slavery.

It is characteristic of a Pauline letter to close with a series of short commands which often include teachings on prayer (see, for example, Rom 15:30–33; 2 Cor 13:7–9; Phil 4:4–7; 1 Thess 5:16–18, 23, 25). The general teaching on prayer here is that it should be constant, with thanksgiving, and for the church's mission. The final three imperatives (3:5–6) are that the Colossian Christians should conduct themselves wisely toward outsiders, make the most of the time, and let their speech be gracious. Each is important to how Christianity would be viewed by outsiders.

REFLECTION ON THE PASSAGE

Colossians 3:18—4:1 seems odd in its context. We've been noting how carefully organized Colossians is and how the author has created "hinge verses" that hold the parts of the letter together. Recall that 3:12–17 are commands to the baptized; 4:2–6 are the same sort of material. You could read from 3:17 to 4:2 and not note that anything was missing. This leads biblical scholars to suggest that 3:18—4:1 is an insertion. The author has "inserted" or introduced another sort of material at this point.

It was a recognizable sort of material to the letter's first recipients, just as "Dear Abby" letters were a recognizable sort of literature to my generation of newspaper readers. What we have here is called a "household code," a *Haustafel* in German. In secular literature in the Greco-Roman period, especially in the writings of the moralists, one finds advice for families. The moralists note the kinds of relationships within a household or extended family (as most families were in the period) and give advice for how they should conduct themselves toward one another. How should wives and husbands, parents and children, slaves and masters behave toward each other were important questions because, for example, Aristotle's assumption was (and I dare say it is still held by many people) that the order of the family reflects order in the society. Household relations reflect the wider social reality. If individual households were well ordered, then the assumption was that the society itself would function properly. This sort of advice literature was, thus, critically important, and observing its rules had high stakes (for more, see pp. 43–45 above).

One reason we think this literary form was common in the New Testament period is that the early Christian writers developed and used it frequently. We find it not only here in Colossians, but in greatly expanded form in Eph 5:21—6:9, and also in 1 Pet

3:1–7. I stress the point about literary form because some people who read or interpret these passages get stuck on the "wives be subject to your husbands" part (3:18) and miss the larger point of the whole passage. There *are* appropriate and inappropriate ways for people to behave toward one another. That's why periodical columns and books on "relationship advice" are still popular. We want to figure out the "right way" to do things.

The New Testament household codes present pairs of relationships: husbands/wives; fathers/children; masters/slaves with a discernible pattern. A party is addressed (wives); a command is given (be subject to your husbands); the theological reason for the action is given (as is fitting in the Lord). Children—obey your parents—this is your acceptable duty in the Lord. You see the pattern. What is striking about the *Christian* use of this form is its reciprocity and the theological motivations given for action. Generally speaking, it's not just the subordinate member of the pair (wives, children, slaves) that are given instructions, but the "power person" (husband, father, master who is likely to be the same person) is also reminded that he, too, has responsibilities to treat people "justly and fairly" since he, too, has "a Master in heaven" (4:1). The male in the Christian family, the equivalent of the Roman *paterfamilias*, is commanded to be loving to his wife, patient and kind to his children, just and fair with his slaves (an institution assumed in the New Testament world and by Jesus, but, thankfully, now almost universally forbidden by law).

So why does the author insert relationship advice into his letter to the Colossians? To prevent persecution and to evangelize. In many of his letters, Paul evinces an interest in marriage and family. First Corinthians 7 is perhaps the most extended passage on the subject. As an educated Greco-Roman Jew, Paul's interest in the family is a specific instance of his more general concern with order. "God," he wrote to the Corinthians, "is a God not of disorder but of peace" (1 Cor 14:33). Thus, "all things should be done decently and in order" (1 Cor 14: 40). For Paul, order reflects the nature of God. It should not be surprising to find Paul's assumptions in his disciples and those who taught after him.

We already know something about why family order was important at the time. But order in the *Christian* family was even more important both because it is godly to be orderly, and it is a way to refute those who criticized Christianity, indeed even accused Christians of being deviant. The author of Colossians wants to minimize what Margaret MacDonald in her commentary called "controversial visibility"[178] on the part of Christians. In some ways 4:5 "conduct yourselves wisely toward outsiders," is the principle behind every instruction from 3:1 on. The author wants the Christians in Colossae to be exemplary in every way, in their personal behavior and in the structure of their families, first, so that Christianity won't be criticized by non-Christians, and second, so that non-Christians will see the order, peace and beauty of Christian lives and want to join their fellowship. He is both trying to protect the Colossian Christians from persecution and further to evangelize in Colossae.

Colossians 3:18—4:6 speaks to a basic tension in Christian life between inner and outer, personal and public, church and society. In the inner and personal realm 3:18b speaks not only to wives, but to every Christian: husbands, parents, children, workers, whomever we are, our behavior must be "fitting in the Lord." Repeatedly in Colossians, the author has reminded Christians that they live "in the Lord." This is the Christian's private, interior reality. And his or her outer behavior should reflect it. All of us should be ordered people, loving, patient, good workers, just and fair. We should do what we do, everything we do, "as for the Lord" (3:23). It is how we serve Jesus. As Br. Lawrence wrote so long ago in *The Practice of the Presence of God* we can be as close to God scrubbing pots in the kitchen as on our knees in church when we do everything "as for the Lord."[179]

Living and working to please the Lord, having that desire as the basic motivation in life, has an external effect. It is how we "conduct ourselves wisely toward outsiders" (4:5). And it is how, as the author well knew, God opens "a door for the word, that we may declare the mystery of Christ" to outsiders (4:3). Whether we like it or not, people look at Christians, and they draw conclusions about Christ. How we conduct our public lives is our most potent evangelistic outreach. This gives me, and I suspect some of you, as well, great pause. The Colossians letter is interested in how Christians lived their lives in the Lord because how they did that basically determined how they related to outsiders, and how they related to outsiders determined both their own safety in a pagan society *and* how Christianity would be viewed and would expand *in* that society.

In this regard, things haven't changed very much since the end of the first century AD. On our personal behavior hangs the fate of our families. And still in some ways, on our families hangs the fate of our society. What we often think of as our "private actions" have both public and eternal consequences for us and for our world. Little wonder the author closes this section of the letter with the command to devote ourselves to prayer.

14

No Lone Rangers

(4:2–18)

TEXTUAL NOTES

Colossians 4:2–6 are in literary form *topoi* (on prayer, vv. 2–4, and on conduct toward those outside the Christian community, vv. 5–6) and have been treated elsewhere in this book (pp. 72–80 above). Greetings from those with Paul and from the apostle to a letter's recipients are also a standard feature of his letters. Colossians 4:7–17 greets ten people by name. Eight names are of those with the author. One is to the woman Nympha who leads a house church, and one is an admonition to a worker to complete his task. Two of these are the author's emissaries, and the names suggest that only three are fellow Jews ("ones of the circumcision among my co-workers," 4:11) These closing greetings, like those in Paul's uncontested letters, suggest the author's gift for friendship, provide information about his mission, help to establish his authority to carry it out, and introduce his fellow-workers, both men and women. (For full treatment of this material, see pp. 54–62 above.)

Verse 18 is an unusually brief closing. It suggests (as did the opening formula) that Paul is the letter's author and has written in his own hand (that is, not used scribes some of whom are introduced in other letters of the Pauline corpus). The repeated allusion to imprisonment (1:24–2:5; 4:3) serves to reinforce the author's (if it is not Paul) authority and to exert the sort of "emotional blackmail" we find in Paul's letter to Philemon and to the Philippian church. The grace wish is offered without reference or allusion to Jesus, perhaps for the same reason it is omitted in the greeting (1:2). Directly or by allusion, the whole letter has been about the grace of Jesus Christ.

REFLECTION ON THE PASSAGE

When I say "the Apostle Paul," what image comes to mind? An old man? A young man? Bearded? Kind? Fiery? Gentle? Critical? And when I say "the Pauline Mission" what image comes to mind? Paul tramping alone along a dusty road in Asia Minor? Paul on a ship being tossed in a Mediterranean storm? Paul in a terrible dungeon? Paul preaching on the Areopagus, on steps of a synagogue somewhere in the Roman Empire?

Do we picture Paul working as a solitary figure? If so we ignore the evidence of the New Testament. Almost immediately after his conversion, Paul is brought to the church in Damascus by Ananias and, later, is ordained in Antioch with Barnabas. He traveled with Barnabas and Mark and Timothy. Paul's missionary method was to go into a city and gather up the already existing Christians to help him. When he moved on, it was after he had organized the local house churches and established relationships with their leaders, a number of whom (as in the Colossian area, 4:15) were women.

Paul wrote to those he'd left behind. Many of Paul's letters were co-authored by Timothy and Sosthenes. At the end of most of his letters there are greetings (and often instructions) to many people he knows. It's a feature of the Pauline letter structure, one clearly in evidence in Colossians whether the author is Paul or one of his disciples. Tychicus, Onesimus (the slave about whom the letter to Philemon is written), Mark, Jesus Justus, Epaphras (founder of the Colossian church whose authority Paul supports), Luke,

Demas, Nympha (the woman who leads a house church), Archippus. We don't know much about these people except that they were *synergos*, fellow workers with Paul in the Gospel. In her commentary, Margaret MacDonald notes "this term stresses mutual reliance and the collaborative nature of the Pauline mission."[180] They needed Paul; Paul needed them. Paul's work was collaborative.

The Colossian church needed Pauline teaching as it faced the challenge of false teachers. They needed the letter's author to remind them of the meaning and power of their baptisms and of the supremacy of Christ in the universe created by and for and through him. They needed him to support the authority of their leader, Epaphras, who is his "beloved fellow slave" (1:7), who brought them the gospel, who wrestles (the English word does not convey the power of the Greek) in his prayers on their behalf.

The letter's author needs the Colossians. He needs their church to be an outpost of the truth of the Gospel that he received from Paul and preaches. He needs each Colossian Christian to live in such a way that non-Christians in Colossae will see their peaceful and ordered lives and want to become slaves of their great Master, Jesus the Christ of God. The author needs the Colossians to spread the message of Jesus Christ. He needs them to support him in prayer, and he asks for their prayers and promises them his own. Paul and the author of Colossians were human beings. And human beings need to be appreciated for their work and for who they are. Paul and the author of Colossians needed his churches for that, too.

As we have considered the Colossian letter, we've noted how it has focused on the communal nature of Christian faith. "You" in the letter is most often second person plural (the "ya'll" of the south or the "y'uns" of Pittsburgh). The thanksgiving and prayer in 1:3-12 is for the whole community. The author speaks of their pagan past and communal estrangement from God which is overcome in Jesus Christ in whom "the whole fullness of deity dwells" (2:9). He doesn't want the community led astray by plausible, but false arguments for "life style choices" that "are of no value" (2:23) to those who "have been raised with Christ" and who are to seek and live His risen life (3:1). The author wants to build up a community, so he tells them that ethnic (Greek and Jew), religious (circumcised and uncircumcised), and economic (slave and free) distinctions are obliterated in Christ. He reminds them to "bear with one another," to "forgive each other" (3:13), to be bound together in love. When the "peace of Christ" rules in individual hearts and "the word of Christ" dwells richly therein this is possible in any community.

Like this author and the Colossian Christians to whom he writes, we cannot make it alone. We were never intended to do so. We were made to live together. The book of Genesis suggests that Adam in the glory of the Garden of Eden got lonely so God made Eve. In fact, one of the things that Christians assert most distinctively is that *God* is essentially a *relationship*: three persons: Father, Son, Spirit or Creator, Redeemer, Sustainer (Those where the same assertions of the Christ hymn in 1:15–20.). If the God in whose image we are made is relational, it's logical that we would be made for relationship, for each other.

Unfortunately, the American national myth gets this wrong. We are great individualists. As early as the eighteenth century. a Frenchman, Alex de Tocqueville, noticed this about us. You know the basic pattern of the American story: a single individual vs. the continent, a man vs. nature. A lone family comes into the Ohio Valley in the eighteenth century and hacks a farm out of the wilderness above the river. The Lone Ranger rescues all the maidens and catches all the cattle thieves West of the Mississippi River while Tonto stands quietly by and grunts "Go, Kemosabe." Except it wasn't like this, as the forts along the Ohio River like the one in Steubenville, Ohio, or the wagon trains that moved people westward, or all our tiny villages with frontier beginnings attest.

This myth, this story we tell to explain who we are, has infected our stance toward other nations in the world. This was brought vividly home to me when I preached on Philippians to a large congregation in Arizona and mentioned that Paul said "our citizenship is in heaven" (3:20), and I used the perhaps unfortunate phrase "an illegal war." After the service a man came up and soundly criticized me. When I quietly reminded him in a certain action America was not in compliance with international law or the rulings of the world court, he said "We're Americans. They don't apply to us." This is the attitude of many American Christians.

We have thought we could make it on our own, standing alone against those we considered enemies of democracy. We thought we had enough human and especially natural resources to do so. Unfortunately, the down turns in our economy and repeated oil crises and illness that quickly jumps national boarders suggest otherwise. And so does international terrorism. This letter's author needed the Colossians, and the Colossians needed him. The world needs America, and America needs the rest of the world. We need each other. And, increasingly we are learning the difficult lesson that the various branches of the human family can't make it on their own.

We need each other. There's not a person who will read this book who hasn't really needed someone else at some point in life. When one of us is sick and in hospital, he really needs our prayers, and their family members need our practical support. When one of us is lonely or depressed, she needs a call or a card or a big chocolate cake! When one of us is summoned Home, and there's a wake and a funeral, the bereaved need the community to gather and remember and pray and eat together as token of that Great Reunion Feast that awaits us—us, together. We all desperately need the opportunity both to be loved and, more importantly, to *be* loving. The witness of the New Testament is that's much more important than being loved.

Colossians makes it very clear that we Christians are baptized into Christ Jesus. We live our lives in him, and, astonishingly, the writer tells the Colossians that Christ lives his risen life in them (and thus in us). Wonderful. But the implication of our being children of God in Christ is that we have all these *siblings*. In the reality of the spiritual life that is our authentic and eternal life, we are brothers and sisters to one another with all the rights and responsibilities pertaining thereunto. Margaret MacDonald gets it just right when she reminds us that Col 4:7–18 "offers us a window into a collaborative enterprise—Pauline Christianity."[181] We need each other. And, thanks be to God, here we can be.

ENDNOTES

1. Dunn, *Epistles to the Colossians and to Philemon*, 19.

2. Lohse, *Colossians and Philemon*, 4.

3. D'Angelo, "Colossians."

4. Reno in Seitz, *Colossians*, 14.

5. Seitz, *Colossians*, 19.

6. Ibid., 20.

7. Quoted in Dunn, *Epistles to the Colossians and to Philemon*, 21.

8. Cicero, *Pro Flacco* xxviii.68.

9. Josephus, *Antiquities* 12:149.

10. Quoted in R. P. Martin, *Ephesians, Colossians, and Philemon*, 82. For an excellent discussion of the Jewish community in the area see Dunn, *Epistles to the Colossians and to Philemon*, 23–35.

11. Arnold, "Colossae," 1089.

12. See Lightfoot, *Saint Paul's Epistles*.

13. Dunn, *Epistles to the Colossians and to Philemon*, 23.

14. Furnish, "Colossians, Epistle to the," 1090.

15. Dunn, *Epistles to the Colossians and to Philemon*, 24.

ENDNOTES

16. Ibid., 29–33.

17. Koester, *Introduction to the New Testament*.

18. See Thurston, *Reading Colossians, Ephesians and 2 Thessalonians*.

19. For an excellent collection of essays on the methodology by which scholars seek to isolate the "Colossian heresy" see Francis and Meeks, eds., *Conflict at Colossae*.

20. Hooker, "Were There False Teachers in Colossae?" For an excellent summary of the various positions vis à vis the "Colossian heresy" or "false teachers," see Bruce, "The Colossian Heresy."

21. Seitz, *Colossians*, 119 and 121.

22. Ibid., 119.

23. Dunn, *Epistles to the Colossians and to Philemon*, 41.

24. Lohse, *Colossians and Philemon*, 20.

25. Ibid., 3.

26. Ibid., 3–4.

27. Sumney, *Colossians*, vii–viii.

28. See Lohse, *Colossians and Philemon*; or Cope, "On Re-thinking the Philemon-Colossians Connection."

29. For helpful discussions of deutero-Pauline Christianity see Brown, *An Introduction to the New Testament*, chapter 25; and Duling and Perrin, *The New Testament*, chapter 8.

30. Dunn, *Epistles to the Colossians and to Philemon*, 19.

31. A balanced discussion of this is Sumney's, "Those Who 'Pass Judgment.'"

32. See Vawter, "The Colossian Hymn and the Principle of Redaction." A full history of interpretation to the mid-1960s is found in Gabathuler, *Jesus Christus, Haupt de Kirche-Haupt der Welt*.

33. Helpful general articles on the hymn include Robinson, "A Formal Analysis of Colossians 1:15-20"; Wright, "Poetry and Theology in Col. 1:15-20"; R. P. Martin, "An Early Christian Hymn (Col. 1:15-20)."

34. F. C. Burney called the hymn a rabbinic-style meditation on Genesis 1 and Proverbs 8. See "Christ as the ΑΡΧΗ of Creation." An interesting expansion of this is De Maris, *The Colossian Controversy*. For more on Wisdom traditions in the hymn see Balchin, "Paul, Wisdom and Christ"; Glasson, "Colossians 1:18, 15 and Sirach 24"; Hengel, "Jesus as the Messianic Teacher of Wisdom and the Beginnings of Christology," chapter 2; Wilken ed., *Aspects of Wisdom in Judaism and Early Christianity*.

35. For discussions of structure see Bruce, "The 'Christ Hymn' of Colossians 1:15-20"; and McCowan, "The Hymnic Structure of Col 1:15-20."

36. Dunn's reading of 1:15 in *Epistles to Colossians and Philemon*, 87-90, is particularly helpful. And see also Yates, "Colossians 2:15: Christ Triumphant." For more on *archai*, see Carr, *Angels and Principalities*.

37. For more on this point, see House, "The Doctrine of Christ in Colossians."

38. For an interesting study on the word see Overfield, "Pleroma."

39. For more on *pleroma* see Lohse, *Colossians and Philemon*, 56-58; and Overfield, "Pleroma."

40. R. P. Martin's "Reconciliation and Forgiveness" is a particularly full and enlightening treatment.

41. Dunn, *Epistles to Colossians and Philemon*, 86.

42. An older article by Beasley-Murray gives a particularly balanced and helpful reading of this material; see "The Second Chapter of Colossians."

43. Craddock provides a very helpful gloss on this in "'All Things in Him.'"

44. Hendricks, "'All in All': Theological Themes in Colossians," 31.

45. See, for example, Lohse *Colossians and Philemon*, 68-72 and Pokorný, *Colossians*, 96-97.

46. There are in Second Timothy, the most personal of thePastoral Epistles, many parallels with the contents of Colossians and a similar question

about authorship. A full study of this matter has not to my knowledge been undertaken.

47. For more on this point see MacDonald, *Colossians and Ephesians*, 78–79.

48. Sumney, "'I Fill Up What Is Lacking in the Afflictions of Christ'"; and Sumney, *Colossians*, 96–102.

49. Sumney, *Colossians*, 98.

50. Dunn, *Epistles to the Colossians and to Philemon*, 114.

51. MacDonald, *Colossians and Ephesians*, 79. I highly recommend the "Interpretation" essay on 1:24—2:7 in this commentary, 89–95.

52. Bruce, *Epistles to the Colossians, to Philemon and to the Ephesians*, 82.

53. For succinct summaries of various readings see Sumney *Colossians*, 99–101; and Sumney, "'I Fill Up What Is Lacking in the Afflictions of Christ,'" 665. Also of interest is Perriman, "The Pattern of Christ's Sufferings," 62–79.

54. Sumney, *Colossians: A Commentary*, 101.

55. Sumney, "I Fill Up What Is Lacking in the Afflictions of Christ,'" 673. My summary here is taken from Sumney's commentary and article. See note 53 above.

56. *Christian Prayer*, 1262.

57. Sumney, *Colossians*, 143.

58. Dunn, *Epistles to Colossians and Philemon*, 164. For a summary of the interpretations of the word, see Yates, "Colossians 2:14."

59. Sumney, *Colossians*, 144.

60. MacDonald, *Colossians and Ephesians*, 102. Note that the term is also found in the LXX in Tobit 5:3 and 9:5.

61. Blanchette, "Does the Cheirographon of Col. 2:14 Represent Christ Himself?"

62. Quoted in Weiss, "The Law in the Epistle to the Colossians," 302.

63. For more on the idea of the "book of guilt," see Dunn, *Epistles to Colossians and Philemon*, 164–66; Sumney, *Colossians*, 144–45; and Pokorny, *Colossians*, 138.

64. MacDonald, *Colossians and Ephesians*, 102–3 and 107–8.

65. R. P. Martin, "Reconciliation and Forgiveness," 120–23.

66. Ibid., 123.

67. The definitive work on the triumphal process is Hafemann's *Suffering and the Spirit*. And see also Duff, "Metaphor, Motif, and Meaning"; Thurston, "2 Corinthians 2:14–16a"; and Williamson, "Led in Triumph," 317–22.

68. Dunn, *Epistles to Colossians and Philemon* 166 and quotation from 170.

69. The exact meaning of the term which appears in Gal 4:3 and 9 and Col 2:8 and 20, is energetically debated. It seems to mean "elementary things" understood as "elemental spirits of the world," cosmic powers that controlled the universe or as the basic elements (earth, air, fire, water) or as rudimentary religious observances. For more see the excursus in Lohse, *Colossians and Philemon*, 96–99; Dunn, *The Epistles to Colossians and Philemon*, 148–51; MacGregor, "Principalities and Powers"; and Weiss, "The Law in the Epistle to the Colossians," 294–99.

70. Sumney, *Colossians*, 148.

71. Yates, "The Christian Way of Life," 241.

72. See, for example, material on this matter in Selwyn, *First Epistle of Peter*.

73. Moule, "'The New Life,'" 242 and 244.

74. Hendricks argues that the Colossian "heresy" was adding requirements to the essential message of Christ; see "'All in All:' Theological Themes in Colossians," 23–35, esp. 29.

75. Hinson, "The Christian Household in Col 3:18–4:1," 496.

76. Cannon, *Use of Traditional Materials in Colossians*.

77. Ibid., 49.

78. Yates, The Christian Way of Life," 246. An accessible introduction to the subject is L. Martin, *Hellenistic Religions*. Fuller accounts include Klauck, *Religious Context of Early Christianity*; and Koester, *Introduction to the New Testament*, vol 1.

79. See, for example, Rom 1:29–31; 1 Cor 5:10–11; 2 Cor 12:21; Gal 5:19–21. An older, but very helpful overview of the form is found in Easton, "New Testament Ethical Lists," 1–2.

80. Cannon, *The Use of Traditional Materials*, 64.

81. For more on the Scythians, see Sumney, *Colossians*, 208–9.

82. For more on forgiveness in Colossians, see Martin, "Reconciliation and Forgiveness."

83. See chapter 4 on "The Name" in Thurston, *Spiritual Life in the Early Church*.

84. For more see Bradley, "The *Topos* as a Form in Pauline Paraenesis."

85. Crouch, *Origin and Intention of the Colossian Haustafel*.

86. Levine, ed., *Feminist Companion to the Deutero-Pauline Epistles*.

87. Osiek and Balch, *Families in the New Testament World*; and see also Lefkowitz and Fant, *Women's Life in Greece and Rome*.

88. Cannon, *Use of Traditional Materials*, discusses the point on 109–22 and concludes that the form originated with the early Church but was influenced by other contemporary teaching forms. And see C. J. Martin, "The *Haustafeln*," 208–9.

89. See *Politics* 1:1245b.

90. Hinson, "The Christian Household," 496.

91. Cannon, *Use of Traditional Materials*, 98.

92. C. J. Martin, "The *Haustafeln*," 208.

93. Bartchy, *First-century Slavery*; and Bartchy, "Slavery, New Testament."

94. C. J. Martin, The *Haustafeln*," 211–12.

95. Rienecker and Rogers, *Linguistic Key to the Greek New Testament*, 584. For an applied theology of time see Thurston, *To Everything a Season*.

96. Lohse, *Colossians and Philemon*, 3.

97. Ibid.

98. An earlier version of this chapter appeared in *Restoration Quarterly* 41 (1999) 45–53. I am grateful to the editors for permission to use that material here.

99. See the Pauline material in Thurston, *Women in the New Testament*; the popular article, Thurston, "Paul: The Misunderstood Apostle"; and Thurston, "Women in the New Testament."

100. For full discussions of Hellenistic letter writing see Murphy-O'Connor, *Paul the Letter Writer*; Stowers, *Letter Writing in Greco-Roman Antiquity*; and on formulae in the letters, Mullins, "Formulas in New Testament Epistles."

101. Material in this paragraph follows that in Mullins, "Greeting as a New Testament Form."

102. Lohse, *Colossians and Philemon*, 172.

103. For more see Thurston, *Reading Colossians, Ephesians and 2 Thessalonians*.

104. See, for example, Bruce, *The Pauline Circle*; Hiebert, *Personalities around Paul*; Ladd, "Paul's Friends in Colossians 4:7–16"; Redlich, *Paul and His Companions*; Robertson, *Some Minor Characters in the New Testament*.

105. Lohse *Colossians and Philemon*, 171. Lightfoot raises the question whether Tychicus was a minister to the churches or to Paul himself. See Lightfoot, *St Paul's Epistles to the Colossians and Philemon*, 234. For a discussion of the terms used in connection with Paul's co-workers, see Ellis, "Paul and His Co-Workers."

106. Lightfoot suggests that the term was a customary form of address of bishops speaking of deacons in the early church. Lightfoot, *Paul's Epistles to the Colossians and Philemon*, 234.

107. Bruce, *The Pauline Circle*, 81.

108. Patzia, *Ephesians, Colossians and Philemon*, 133.

109. Pokorny, *Colossians*, 191.

110. For fuller discussion of Onesimus, see Bruce, *Paul, Apostles of the Heart Set Free*, chapter 34; Bruce, *Pauline Circle*, chapter 9; Harrison, "Onesimus and Philemon"; Petersen, *Rediscovering Paul*.

111. For more see Barclay, "Paul, Philemon and the Dilemma of Christian Slave Ownership."

112. For more on slavery generally, see Bartchy, *First-Century Slavery and 1 Corinthians 7:21*; and Bartchy, "Slavery, NT," which has a good bibliography. Also of interest are Buckland, *The Roman Law of Slavery*; Finley, *Ancient Slavery and Modern Ideology*; and Westermann, *The Slave Systems of Greek and Roman Antiquity*. For a clear discussion of slavery in Philemon, see Barclay, "Paul, Philemon and the Dilemma of Christian Slave Ownership."

113. For more information on what this means see Ellis, "'Those of the Circumcision' and the Early Christian Mission."

114. For discussions of the term see Harris, *Colossians and Philemon*, 206; Lightfoot, *Paul's Epistles to the Colossians and Philemon*, 236; Lohse, *Colossians and Philemon*, 173; and Moule, *Epistles of Paul the Apostle to the Colossians and to Philemon*, 137.

115. For a full discussion of Barnabas, see Bruce *The Pauline Circle*, chapter 2.

116. For a fuller discussion of the terms, see Furnish, "'Fellow Workers in God's Service.'"

117. Lohse, *Colossians and Philemon*, 172.

118. Lightfoot, *Paul's Epistles to the Colossians and Philemon*, 239; and Lohse *Colossians and Philemon*, 173 and n. 29.

119. Lightfoot provides a full exposition of the term in ibid., 240.

120. See Olson, "Pauline Expressions of Confidence in His Addressees."

121. For a fuller discussion see Bruce *The Pauline Circle*, chapter 5.

122. Anderson, "Who Wrote the Epistle from Laodicea?"

123. Malherbe, *Social Aspects of Early Christianity*.

124. Abbott, *Epistle to the Ephesians and to the Colossians*, 303–4; Lightfoot, *St. Paul's Epistles to the Colossians and Philemon*, 242.

125. Moulton, "Nympha."

126. Lightfoot, *St. Paul's Epistles to the Colossians and Philemon*, 243.

127. Schweizer, *Letter to the Colossians*, 24; and see Lohse, *Colossians and Philemon*, 174.

128. So Pokorný, *Colossians*, 195.

129. See Brooten, "Junia . . . Outstanding among the Apostles."

130. SeeThurston, *Widows*; and Thurston, "1 Timothy 5:3–16 and Leadership of Women in the Early Church."

131. For an alternative reading of the textual evidence see R. P. Martin, *Colossians and Philemon*, 136–37.

132. See Knox, *Philemon among the Letters of Paul.*

133. The case for Knox's argument has been strengthened by a careful exegetical note Cope, "On Re-thinking the Philemon-Colossians Connection."

134. Abbott, *The Epistle to the Ephesians and to the Colossians*, 307.

135. Bruce, *The Epistles to the Colossians, to Philemon, and to the Ephesians*, 185.

136. Lohse, *Colossians and Philemon*, 177.

137. Excellent studies of the Greco-Roman letter include Murphy-O'Connor, *Paul the Letter Writer*; and White, *Light from Ancient Letters*. And see note 147 below.

138. Rienecker and Rogers, *Linguistic Key to the Greek New Testament*, 564.

139. For more see Thurston, "Prayer in the New Testament."

140. Van Elderen, "The Verb in the Epistolary Invocation."

141. For more on this see Harrelson, "Blessings and Curses."

142. Sumney, *Colossians*, 28.

143. MacDonald, *Colossians and Ephesians*, 31.

144. Stanley, *Boasting in the Lord*, especially chapter 3, sec. 4.

145. Jewett, "The Form and Function of the Homiletic Benediction."

146. Stowers, *Letter Writing in Greco-Roman Antiquity*.

147. There is an extensive literature on the opening prayer in Pauline letters. The seminal study is Schubert, *Form and Function of the Pauline Thanksgiving*. See also O'Brien, *Introductory Thanksgivings in the Letters of Paul*; O'Brien, "Thanksgiving and the Gospel in Paul"; White, "Introductory Formulae in the Body of a Pauline Letter"; and Wiles, *Paul's Intercessory Prayers*.

148. Sumney, *Colossians*, 34.

149. Ibid., 41.

150. O'Brien, "Thanksgiving and the Gospel in Paul," 149, 153, 155.

151. O'Brien, *Introductory Thanksgivings in the Letters of Paul*, 103.

152. MacDonald, *Colossians and Ephesians*, 49.

153. Ibid., 54.

154. Christopher Seitz draws out the Old Testament implications of inheritance language in *Colossians*, 82–83.

155. MacDonald, *Colossians and Ephesians*, 57.

156. Sumney, *Colossians*, 256.

157. Epictetus, *Diatr.* 2.1.19, quoted in Sumney, *Colossians*, 257.

158. Stanley, *Boasting in the Lord*, 147.

159. Steindl-Rast, *Gratefulness*.

160. Burrows, *The Essence of Prayer*, 5–6.

161. This idea is treated extensively in Frenette, *The Path of Centering Prayer.*

162. See, for example, Schweizer, "Christ in the Letter to the Colossians"; O'Neill, "The Source of Christology in Colossians."

163. For a succinct presentation of theology in Colossians see Lohse, "Pauline Theology in the Letter to the Colossians."

164. Wright, "Poetry and Theology in Col. 1:15–20," 461. I have paraphrased his remark. And see also House, "The Doctrine of Christ in Colossians."

165. Steindl-Rast and Grun, *Faith Beyond Belief.*

166. Ibid. Br. David also reminds us that Augustine compares the Father to the Logos, the Holy Spirit of silence and understanding. It was profoundly moving for this writer and poet to imagine God as Silence from which come the Word (Christ) who is understood by means of the Holy Spirit (the force of understanding.) See ibid., 76–77.

167. Burrows, *The Essence of Prayer*, 31.

168. Pokorný, *Colossians*, 95.

169. Dunn, *The Epistles to the Colossians and to Philemon*. And see Rom 1:11–15; 1 Thess 2:17—3:11; and especially Gal 1:10—2:21.

170. In a Bible study I taught on Colossians, one gentleman pointed out that only a Jewish scholar like Paul *could* convincingly teach the astonishing truth of God's inclusion of non-Jews as "chosen ones."

171. De Caussade, *Abandonment to Divine Providence*, 36.

172. Ellsberg, ed., *Charles de Foucauld*, 108–9.

173. See Käsemann, "A Primitive Christian Baptismal Liturgy."

174. MacDonald, *Colossians and Ephesians.*

175. Gardner and MacKenzie, eds., *The Poems of Gerard Manley Hopkins*, 63 ("Wreck of the Deutschland," stanza 35)

176. Boulding, *Marked for Life*, 90.

177. Quoted in Steindl-Rast and Grun, *Faith Beyond Belief: Spirituality for Our Times*, 129.

178. MacDonald, *Colossians and Ephesians*, 162.

179. Br. Lawrence of the Resurrection, *The Practice of the Presence of God*.

180. MacDonald, *Colossians and Ephesians*, 181.

181. Ibid., 188.

Bibliography

Abbott, T. K. *The Epistles to the Ephesians and to the Colossians.* New York: Scribner, 1909.

Anderson, Charles P. "Who Wrote the Epistle from Laodicea?" *Journal of Biblical Literature* 85 (1966) 436–40.

Arnold, Clinton E. "Colossae." In *Anchor Bible Dictionary*, edited by David Noel Freedman, 1:1089–90. New York: Doubleday, 1992.

Balchin, John F. "Paul, Wisdom, and Christ." In *Christ the Lord*, edited by Harold H. Rowdon, 204–19. Leicster, UK: InterVarsity, 1982.

Banks, Robert, ed. *Reconciliation and Hope: New Testament Essays on Atonement and Eschatology Presented to L. L. Morris on His 60th Birthday.* Grand Rapids: Eerdmans, 1974.

Barclay, John M. G. "Paul, Philemon and the Dilemma of Christian Slave Ownership." *New Testament Studies* 37 (1991) 161–85.

Bartchy, S. Scott. *First-Century Slavery and 1 Corinthians 7:21.* Society of Biblical Literature Dissertation Series 11. 1973. Reprinted, Eugene, OR: Wipf & Stock, 2003.

———. "Slavery, New Testament." In *Anchor Bible Dictionary*, edited by David Noel Freedman, 6:65–73. New York: Doubleday, 1992.

Beasley-Murray, George R. "The Second Chapter of Colossians." *Review & Expositor* 70 (1973) 469–79.

Blanchette, O. A. "Does the Cheirographon of Col. 2:14 Represent Christ Himself?" *Catholic Biblical Quarterly* 23 (1961) 306–12.

Boulding, Maria. *Marked for Life: Prayer in the Easter Christ.* London: SPCK, 1979.

Bradley, David G., "The *Topos* as Form in Pauline Paraenesis." *Journal of Biblical Literature* 72 (1953) 238–46.

Brooten, Bernadette. "Junia . . . Outstanding among the Apostles." In *Women Priests: A Catholic Commentary on the Vatican Declaration*, edited by Leonard Swidler and Arlene Swidler, 141–44. New York: Paulist, 1977.

Brown, Raymond E. *An Introduction to the New Testament.* Anchor Bible Reference Library. New York: Doubleday, 1997.

Bruce, F. F. "The 'Christ Hymn' of Colossians 1:15–20." *Bibliotheca Sacra* 141 (1984) 99–111.

———. "The Colossian Heresy." *Bibliotheca Sacra* 141 (1984) 195–208.

———. *The Epistles to the Colossians, to Philemon and to the Ephesians.* New International Commentary on the New Testament. Grand Rapids: Eerdmans, 1984.

———. *Paul: Apostle of the Heart Set Free.* Grand Rapids: Eerdmans, 1975.

———. *The Pauline Circle.* Grand Rapids: Eerdmans, 1985.

Buckland, W. W. *The Roman Law of Slavery: The Condition of the Slave in Private Law from Augustus to Justinian.* Cambridge: Cambridge University Press, 1908.

Burney, F. C. "Christ as the ARXH of Creation." *Journal of Theological Studies* 27 (1925/26) 160–77.

Burrows, Ruth. *Essence of Prayer.* Mahwah, NJ: Paulist, 2006.

Buttrick, George Arthur, ed. *The Interpreter's Dictionary of the Bible.* Nashville: Abingdon, 1962.

Cannon, George E. *The Use of Traditional Materials in Colossians.* Macon, GA: Mercer University Press, 1983.

Carr, Wesley. *Angels and Principalities: The Background, Meaning and Development of The Pauline Phrase HAI ARCHAI KAN HAI EXOUSIAI.* Society for New Testament Studies Monograph Series 42. Cambridge: Cambridge University Press, 1981.

Christian Prayer: The Liturgy of the Hours. New York: Catholic Book Publishing, 1962.

Cope, Lamar. "On Re-thinking the Philemon-Colossians Connection." *Biblical Research* 30 (1985) 45–50.

Craddock, Fred B. "'All Things in Him': A Critical Note on Col. 1:15–20." *New Testament Studies* 12 (1965–66) 78–80.

Crouch, James E. *The Origin and Intention of the Colossian Haustafel.* Forschungen zur Religion und Literatur des Alten und Neuen Testaments 109. Göttingen: Vandenhoeck & Ruprecht, 1972.

D'Angelo, Mary Rose. "Colossians." In *Searching the Scriptures*, edited by Elisabeth Schüssler Fiorenza, 313–24. New York: Crossroad, 1994.

DeCaussade, Jean-Pierre. *Abandonment to Divine Providence.* Translated by John Beevers. New York: Image, 1975.

De Maris, Richard E. *The Colossian Controversy: Wisdom in Dispute at Colossae.* Journal for the Study of the New Testament Supplement Series 96. Sheffield: JSOT Press, 1994.

Duff, Paul B., "Metaphor, Motif, and Meaning: The Rhetorical Strategy behind the Image 'Led in Triumph' in 2 Corinthians 2:14." *Catholic Biblical Quarterly* 53 (1991) 79–92.

Dulling, Dennis C., and Norman Perrin. The *New Testament: Proclamation and Parenesis, Myth and History.* 3rd ed. New York: Harcourt Brace, 1994.

Dunn, James D. G. *The Epistles to the Colossians and to Philemon*. New International Greek Testament Commentary. Grand Rapids Eerdmans, 1996.

Easton, B. S. "New Testament Ethical Lists." *Journal of Biblical Literature* 51 (1932) 1–12.

Ellsberg, Robert, ed. *Charles de Foucauld: Writings*. Maryknoll, NY: Orbis, 1999.

Ellis, E. Earl. "Paul and His Co-Workers." *New Testament Studies* 17 (1971) 437–52.

————. "'Those of the Circumcision' and the Early Christian Mission." *Studia Evangelium* 4 (1968) 390–99.

Felder, Cain Hope, ed. *Stony the Road We Trod, African-American Biblical Interpretation*. Minneapolis: Fortress, 1991.

Finley, Moses I. *Ancient Slavery and Modern Ideology*. New York: Viking, 1985.

Francis Fred O., and Wayne Meeks, ed. *Conflict at Colossae: A Problem in the Interpretation of Early Christianity, Illustrated by Selected Modern Studies*. Sources for Biblical Study 4. Missoula, MT: Scholars, 1975.

Freedman, David Noel, ed. *The Anchor Bible Dictionary*. 6 vols. New York: Doubleday, 1992.

Furnish, Victor Paul. "Colossians, Epistle to the." In *Anchor Bible Dictionary*, edited by David Noel Freedman, 1:1090–96. New York: Doubleday, 1992.

————. "'Fellow Workers in God's Service.'" *Journal of Biblical Literature* 80 (1961) 364–70.

Gabathuler, Hans Jakob. *Jesus Christus, Haupt de Kirche-Haupt der Welt: Der Christushymnus Colosser 1, 15–20 in der theologischen Forschung der letzten 130 Jahre*. Abhandlungen zur Theologie des Alten und Neuen Testaments 45. Zurich: Zwingli, 1965.

Gardner, W. H., and N. H. MacKenzie. *The Poems of Gerard Manley Hopkins*. 4th ed. Oxford: Oxford University Press, 1970.

Glasson, T. Francis. "Colossians 1:18, 15 and Sirach 24." *Journal of Biblical Literature* 86 (1967) 214–16.

Hafemann, Scott J. *Suffering and the Spirit: An Exegetical Study of 2 Cor. 2:14–3:4*. Tübingen: Mohr/Siebeck, 1986.

Hanson, Stig. *The Unity of the Church in the New Testament: Colossians and Ephesians*. Acta Seminarii neotestamentici upsaliensis 14. Uppsala: Almqvist & Wiksells, 1946.

Harrelson, Walter J. "Blessings and Curses." In *Interpreter's Dictionary of the Bible*, edited by George Arthur Buttrick, 1:446–48. Nashville: Abingdon, 1962.

Harris, Murray J. *Colossians and Philemon*. Exegetical Guide to the Greek New Testament. Grand Rapids: Eerdmans, 1991.

Harrison, P. "Onesimus and Philemon." *Anglican Theological Review* 32 (1950) 168–294.

Hendricks, William L. "'All in All': Theological Themes in Colossians." *Southwestern Journal of Theology* 16 (1973) 23–35.

Hengel, Martin. "Jesus as the Messianic Teacher of Wisdom and the Beginnings of Christology." In *Studies in Early Christology*, 73–117. Edinburgh: T. & T. Clark, 1995.

Hiebert, D. Edmund. *Personalities around Paul*. Chicago: Moody, 1975.

Hinson, E. Glenn. "The Christian Household in Col 3:1841." *Review & Expositor* 70 (1973) 495–507.

Hooker, Morna D. "Were There False Teachers in Colossae?" In *Christ and the Spirit in the New Testament*, edited by Barnabas Lindars and Stephen S. Smalley, 315–31. Cambridge: Cambridge University Press, 1973.

House, H. Wayne. "The Doctrine of Christ in Colossians." *Bibliotheca Sacra* 149 (1992) 180–92.

Jewett, Robert. "The Form and Function of the Homiletic Benediction." *Anglican Theological Review* 51 (1969) 18–34.

Käsemann, Ernst. *Essays on New Testament Themes*. Translated by W. J. Montague. Philadelphia: Fortress, 1964.

Klauck, Hans-Josef. *The Religious Context of Early Christianity: A Guide to Graeco-Roman Religions*. Translated by Brian McNeil. Edinburgh: T. & T. Clark, 2000.

Knox, John. *Philemon among the Letters of Paul*. 2nd ed. Chicago: University of Chicago Press, 1938.

Koester, Helmut. *Introduction to the New Testament*. 2 vols. Philadelphia: Fortress, 1982.

Ladd, George E. "Paul's Friends in Colossians 4:7–16." *Review & Expositor* 70 (1973) 507–14.

Lawrence of the Resurrection, Brother. *The Practice of the Presence of God*. Translated by Sr. Mary David, SSND. New York: Paulist, 1978.

Lefkowitz, Mary R., and Maureen B. Fant. *Women's Life in Greece and Rome*. Baltimore: Johns Hopkins University Press, 1982.

Levine, Amy-Jill, ed. *A Feminist Companion to the Deutero-Pauline Epistles*. Feminist Companion to the New Testament and Early Christian Writings 7. London: T. & T. Clark, 2003.

Lightfoot, J. B. *Paul's Epistles to the Colossians and Philemon*. London: Macmillan, 1882.

Lindars, Barnabas, and Stephen S. Smalley, eds. *Christ and Spirit in the New Testament*. Cambridge: Cambridge University Press, 1973.

Lohse, Eduard. *Colossians and Philemon*. Hermeneia. Philadelphia: Fortress, 1971.

———. "Pauline Theology in the Letter to the Colossians." *New Testament Studies* 15 (1968–69) 211–20.

MacDonald, Margaret Y. *Colossians and Ephesians*. Sacra Pagina 17. Collegeville, MN: Liturgical, 2000.

MacGregor, G. H. C. "Principalities and Powers: The Cosmic Background of Paul's Thought." *New Testament Studies* 1 (1954–55) 17–28.

Malherbe, Abraham J. *Social Aspects of Early Christianity*. 2nd ed., 1983. Reprinted, Eugene, OR: Wipf & Stock, 2003.

Martin, Clarice J. "The *Haustafeln* in African-American Biblical Interpretation: 'Free Slaves' and 'Subordinate Women.'" In *Stony the Road We Trod: African-American Biblical Interpretation*, 206–31. Minneapolis: Fortress, 1991.

Martin, Luther H. *Hellenistic Religions: An Introduction.* New York: Oxford University Press, 1987.

Martin, Ralph P. *Colossians and Philemon.* New Century Bible Commentary. Grand Rapids: Eerdmans, 1985.

———. "An Early Christian Hymn (Col 1:15–20)." *Evangelical Quarterly* 36 (1964) 195–205.

———. *Ephesians, Colossians, and Philemon.* Interpretation. Atlanta: John Knox, 1991.

———. "Reconciliation and Forgiveness in the Letter to the Colossians." In *Reconciliation and Hope: New Testament Essays on Atonement and Eschatology Presented to L. L. Morris on His 60th Birthday*, edited by Robert Banks, 104–24. Grand Rapids: Eerdmans, 1974.

McCowan, Wayne. "The Hymnic Structure of Col 1:15–20." *Evangelical Quarterly* 51 (1979) 156–62.

Moule, C. F. D. *The Epistles to the Colossians and to Philemon.* Cambridge Greek Testament. Cambridge: Cambridge University Press, 1962.

Moulton, James H. "Nympha." *Expository Times* 5 (1893–94) 66–67.

Mullins, Terence Y. "Formulas in New Testament Epistles." *Journal of Biblical Literature* 91 (1972) 380–90.

———. "Greeting as a New Testament Form." *Journal of Biblical Literature* 87 (1968) 418–26.

Murphy-O'Connor, Jerome. *Paul the Letter-Writer: His World, His Options, His Skills.* Good New Studies 41. Collegeville, MN: Liturgical, 1995.

———. "'The New Life' in Colossians 3:1–17." *Review & Expositor* 70 (1973) 481–83.

O'Brien, Peter T. *Introductory Thanksgiving in the Letters of Paul.* Novum Testamentum Supplements 49. Leiden: Brill, 1977.

———. "Thanksgiving and the Gospel in Paul." *New Testament Studies* 21 (1974–75) 144–55.

Olson, Stanley N. "Pauline Expressions of Confidence in His Addressees." *Catholic Biblical Quarterly* 47 (1985) 282–95.

O'Neill, J. C. "The Source of Christology in Colossians." *New Testament Studies* 26 (1979) 87–100.

Osiek, Carolyn, and David L. Balch. *Families in the New Testament World: Households and House Churches.* Family, Religion, and Culture. Louisville: Westminster John Knox, 1997.

Overfield, P. D. "Pleroma: A Study in Content and Context." *New Testament Studies* 25 (1979) 385–96.

Patzia, Arthur G. *Ephesians, Colossians, Philemon.* New International Biblical Commentary 10. Peabody: Hendrickson, 1990.

Perriman, A. "The Pattern of Christ's Sufferings: Col. 1:24 and Phil. 3: 10–11." *Tyndale Bulletin* 42 (1991) 62–79.

Petersen, Norman R. *Rediscovering Paul: Philemon and the Sociology of Paul's Narrative World.* 1985. Reprinted, Eugene, OR: Wipf & Stock, 2008.

Pokorný, Petr. *Colossians: A Commentary.* Translated by Siegfried S. Schatzmann. Peabody: Hendrickson, 1991.

Redlich, Edwin B. *Paul and His Companions.* 1913. Reprinted, Hardpress, 2012.

Rienecker, Fritz. *Linguistic Key to the Greek New Testament.* 2 vols. Translated and revised by Cleon L. Rogers. Grand Rapids: Zondervan, 1976–80.

Robertson, A. T. *Some Minor Characters in the New Testament.* New York: Doubleday, 1928.

Robinson, James M. "A Formal Analysis of Colossians 1:15–20." *Journal of Biblical Literature* 76 (1957) 270–87.

Schubert, Paul. *Form and Function of the Pauline Thanksgivings.* Beihefte zur Zeitschrift für die neutestamentliche Wissenschaft 20. Berlin: Töpelmann, 1939.

Schweizer, Eduard. "Christ in the Letter to the Colossians." *Review & Expositor* 70 (1973) 451–67.

Seitz, Christopher R. *Colossians.* Brazos Theological Commentary. Grand Rapids: Baker, 2014.

Selwyn, Edward Gordon. *The First Epistle of Peter.* 2nd ed. London: Macmillan, 1947.

Stanley, David M. *Boasting in the Lord: The Phenomenon of Prayer in St. Paul.* New York: Paulist, 1973.

Steindl-Rast, David, and Anselm Grun. *Faith Beyond Belief: Spirituality for Our Times. A Conversation.* Translated by Linda M. Maloney. Collegeville, MN: Liturgical, 2016.

Steindl-Rast, David. *Gratefulness: The Heart of Prayer. An Approach to Life in Fullness.* New York: Paulist, 1984.

Stowers, Stanley K. *Letter Writing in Greco-Roman Antiquity.* Library of Early Christianity 5. Philadelphia: Westminster, 1986.

Sumney, Jerry L. *Colossians.* New Testament Library. Louisville: Westminster John Knox, 2008.

———. "'I Fill Up What Is Lacking in the Afflictions of Christ': Paul's Vicarious Suffering in Colossians." *Catholic Biblical Quarterly* 68 (2006) 664–80.

———. "Those Who 'Pass Judgment'—The Identity of the Opponents in Colossians." *Biblica* 74 (1993) 366–88.

Thurston, Bonnie. "1 Timothy 5:3–16 and Leadership of Women in the Early Church." In *A Feminist Companion to the Deutero-Pauline Epistles,* edited by Amy-Jill Levine, 159–74. Feminist Companion to the New Testament and Early Christian Writings 7. London: T. and T. Clark, 2003.

———. "2 Corinthians 2:14–16a: Christ's Incense." *Restoration Quarterly* 29 (1987) 65–69.

———. "Paul: The Misunderstood Apostle." *Presbyterians Today* 90 (2000) 21–22.

———. "Paul's Associates in Colossians 4:7–17." *Restoration Quarterly* 41 (1999) 45–53.

———. "Prayer in the New Testament." In *Prayer from Alexander to Constantine: A Critical Anthology,* edited by Mark Kiley et al., 207–10. New York: Routledge, 1977.

———. *Reading Colossians, Ephesians and 2 Thessalonians.* New York: Crossroad, 1995.

———. *Spiritual Life in the Early Church.* Minneapolis: Fortress, 1993.

———. *To Everything a Season: A Spirituality of Time.* 1999. Reprinted, Eugene, OR: Wipf & Stock, 2004.

———. *The Widows: A Women's Ministry in the Early Church.* Philadelphia: Fortress, 1989.

———. *Women in the New Testament.* 1998. Reprinted, Eugene, OR: Wipf & Stock, 2004.

———. "Women in the New Testament: The Example of Romans 16." In *Scripture as the Soul of Theology,* edited by Edward J. Mahoney, 40–59. Collegville, MN: Liturgical, 2005.

Van Elderen, B. "The Verb in the Epistolary Invocation." *Calvin Theological Journal* 2 (1967) 46–48.

Vawter. Bruce. "The Colossian Hymn and the Principle of Redaction." *Catholic Biblical Quarterly* 33 (1971) 62–81.

Weiss, Herold. "The Law in the Epistle to the Colossians." *Catholic Biblical Quarterly* 42 (1972) 294–314.

White, John L. "Introductory Formulae in the Body of a Pauline Letter." *Journal of Biblical Literature* 90 (1971) 91–97.

———. *Light from Ancient Letters.* Foundations and Facets. Philadelphia: Fortress, 1986.

Wiles, Gordon P. *Paul's Intercessory Prayers: The Significance of the Intercessory Prayer Passages in the Letters of St. Paul.* Society for New Testament Studies Monograph Series 24. Cambridge: Cambridge University Press, 2009.

Wilken, Robert L., ed. *Aspects of Wisdom in Early Christianity.* University of Notre Dame Center for the Study of Judaism and Christianity in Antiquity 1. Notre Dame: Notre Dame University Press, 1975.

Williamson, Lamar. "Led in Triumph." *Interpretation* 22 (1968) 317–22.

Wright, N. T. *Colossians and Philemon.* Tyndale New Testament Commentaries. Grand Rapids: Eerdmans, 1986.

———. "Poetry and Theology in Col 1:15–20." *New Testament Studies* 36 (1990) 444–68.

Yates, Roy. "The Christian Way of Life: The Parenetic Material in Colossians 3:1—4:6." *Evangelical Quarterly* 63 (191) 241–51.

———. "Colossians 2:14: Metaphor of Forgiveness." *Biblica* 71 (1990) 248–59.

———. "Colossians 2:15: Christ Triumphant." *New Testament Studies* 37 (1991) 573–91.

Made in the USA
Middletown, DE
20 June 2018